PRAISE FOR PATRICIA EDGAR

'Patricia is a sort of centurion in her abilities to kick down doors and push walls over...she gets things done.'
Phillip Adams

'With her characteristic passion, Patricia Edgar has exploded the myth that an ageing population is unrelieved bad news for our social and economic future. This book is bursting with intellectual energy: if Edgar's rational arguments don't convince you, her human stories will.'
Hugh Mackay

'A robust, persuasive and passionate look at the benefits of an extended life span.' *Sunday Age*

'Patricia Edgar brilliantly portrays the challenges and, more importantly, the manifold joys of growing older. She dissects the biased and inaccurate attitudes which prevent society from gaining maximum value out of its senior citizens. She highlights the experience, perspective, integrity and wisdom of our elders and introduces us to eight individuals enjoying fulfilling lives towards the end of their journeys—independent, interesting and inspirational people, examples to be emulated. This book is a "must read" for every thinking Australian.' Sir Gustav Nossal

PATRICIA EDGAR is a sociologist, educator, film and television producer, writer, researcher and policy analyst. Through a career spanning four decades she has been at the forefront of media for children nationally and internationally, winning multiple awards for her achievements and programs.

IN PRAISE OF AGEING

IN PRAISE OF AGEING

OF

AGEING

PATRICIA EDGAR

TEXT PUBLISHING
MELBOURNE AUSTRALIA

textpublishing.com.au
The Text Publishing Company
Swann House
22 William Street
Melbourne Victoria 3000
Australia

First published in 2013 by The Text Publishing Company
Reprinted 2013

Cover and page design by WH Chong
Typeset by J&M Typesetting
Printed in Australia by Griffin Press, an Accredited ISO AS/NZS 14001:2004 Environmental Management System printer

National Library of Australia Cataloguing-in-Publication entry
ISBN: 9781922147554 (pbk)
ISBN: 9781922148605 (ebook)
Author: Edgar, Patricia, 1937–
Title: In praise of ageing / by Patricia Edgar.
Subjects: Retirement.
Aging--Anecdotes.
Older people--Anecdotes.
Dewey Number: 306.38

This project has been assisted by the Commonwealth Government through the Australia Council, its arts funding and advisory body.

TO
REG & EVA

CONTENTS

NOT OUT

M Y parents, Eva and Reg Etherington, lived to 89 and 95 respectively, and were in excellent health until their final years. They were active, interested in life around them (particularly their children, grandchildren and great grandchildren) and were good company. I enjoyed seeing them and having them stay. They lived independently in the same house they'd moved into when they married and managed with minimal assistance, without being a burden to the state or to their family. To the extent I thought about ageing, I believed you lived your life until you got sick and then you died, all without too much fuss. I had no real understanding of a prolonged ageing process. Reg and Eva did not seem 'old' to me at 85 and only when their years were very advanced did I observe frailty. My mother fell and lost her confidence and mobility (but never broke a bone) and my father developed mild dementia. Still they managed well: he had the legs and she had the memory.

I only began to think about ageing well after I retired and started to experience the aches and pains that led to a hip replacement. Then I was surprised and outraged when I encountered the prejudice and misguided assumptions expressed in the debate on ageing and its 'imminent burden on society'. Looking back on the lives of my parents and of many of their friends I began to think about what determines the way we live. Why do some people live an active and rewarding long life while others die early or live miserably? Is it simply health that determines how long we live? Is it luck? Is it economics? Or is there a pattern that can be emulated so that many more people can learn and be assisted to live productively and contentedly well into their advancing years?

I looked first at those I knew who were approaching 90. I did not need to look far; the interviews I conducted were with friends, relatives of friends or friends of friends. There was no shortage of people to choose from. I did not go out of my way to find exceptional people but they are all exceptional and there are many more like them. Most readers of this book will know remarkable elders.

I began the interviews before I looked at the research and found that there are, indeed, common characteristics which determine successful ageing. Good health and genes are obviously important but they do not tell the full story. No one goes through life escaping hardships, trauma, grief or significant disappointment but the way we deal with these experiences makes all the difference. Resilience and a positive attitude, the ability to reinvent ourselves as circumstances change over the years, engagement with and interest in people and issues, loving relationships with partners, family and friends, and finding a worthwhile purpose are all critical factors in leading a long, rewarding life.

When I did look at the research I found the facts about ageing actually contradict many of the negative stereotypes. Everyone who lives to a ripe old age has a fascinating story to tell and this story informs the way they live in their final years.

PART ONE

THE
GIFT
OF
AGE

CHAPTER 1

THE SECOND HALF OF LIFE

Not long ago I boarded a tram in the Melbourne suburb of Fitzroy. Seated near the front was a woman who suffered from a mental disorder, and was shouting abuse at every person who passed her by. I sat down with my back to her and slightly inclined my head to glance as she shrieked at us. She saw my move and screamed out, 'Bitch.' Then she took another look at me and added, 'Old bitch.'

The word 'old' is used commonly as a pejorative term. 'You silly old bugger,' was Bob Hawke's riposte to a 74-year-old man who challenged him on the campaign trail in Whyalla in 1989. When I had a hearing test recently I was told by the audiologist that my hearing was diminished, consistent with ageing. 'That's what happens when you are old,' she added matter-of-factly, as if describing a 'condition' akin to a disease.

Ageing can be a humbling experience for those fortunate enough to have survived the accidents and exigencies that befall us in life. We complain about its physical effects but most of us agree 'it's better than the alternative'. In fact, increasing numbers of elders are enjoying their later years in ways which defy the stereotypes. Just as late childhood was categorised as adolescence in the 1950s and understood as a new stage in the life cycle, long-living adults are now redefining the stage of late adulthood and what it means to be 'old'.

We who are old do not see ourselves as society defines us. For many, ageing is a liberating experience; we are consoled for any losses by a new sense of freedom and confidence—we don't fear the future and we don't worry so much about the opinions of others. But persistent assumptions about our incapacity undermine our well-being. The main mantra in the media is: 'Now that they are living longer we can't afford them; they are all going to get sick and be a drain on the rest of society.' While this myth is gathering momentum there is another side to the story. This book is about active, engaged older people who are enjoying their lives and continuing to contribute, but often in ways that our economic system does not recognise. Not everyone will reach this stage of life or be fit enough to enjoy it, but this is the trend. Meanwhile current policies are creating unnecessary problems.

The first time I encountered ageism I was 32 years old, setting up a research study in Darwin on the introduction of television to that city. I was working alone and ventured into a café, where I got into a conversation with a group of young people who were, I guessed, in their late teens and early twenties. The next day I returned to the café to be greeted by one of the same young men, who called out, 'Here's the old bird from the south.' I was affronted by this cheeky youth, who challenged my view of myself.

That, of course, was just the beginning. Women are the target of most acts of discrimination, but men are not spared ageist stereotyping and don't much like it either. When my husband, Don, was taken to hospital by ambulance after smashing his foot in an accident, he overheard a nurse comment, 'We've got an old one out there.' Don was 44 at the time.

Now that I am 76, ageism is endemic to my experience, but sometimes it comes from surprising people. Recently I attended a forum at Melbourne University where the speaker was a famous scientist. After his talk I was asking him about the media's coverage of science when he said, 'Do you use the internet?' He would not have asked that of a young person or even, I imagine, an older man. I was taken aback that a distinguished scientist would hold such ingrained ageist assumptions, but looking old takes you to another country.

My doctor, a woman of 65, was enquiring about how I spend my time and we exchanged details of our interests. She said, 'I like to sit and watch people in cafés. My daughter says to stop staring, it's embarrassing. But I tell her not to worry—people don't notice me staring, I'm invisible.' And she is right. To those younger, we are a separate form of life.

People generally do not look at old people. Simone de Beauvoir, in her seminal book *The Coming of Age*, quotes Lucius Caecilius, a banker who lived in the Roman town of Pompeii: 'What I find most lamentable about old age,' he said, 'is that one feels that now one is repulsive to the young.'

It seems not a lot has changed in our perception of old age. Yet much has changed in the way we age and in our life expectancy. We can't define with any clarity who we regard as old anymore. I feel surprise to read, 'An elderly man was hit by a car', only to discover he was 60 years old and may well have 30 years ahead of him. If the label of 'old' is applied to someone in her fifties as well as to a centenarian, then 'old age' is the longest stage of life.

Old age is not new. There are fabulous ages attributed to figures from the Old Testament. While these may be fanciful, there is still evidence of advanced years in history—the biographer Diogenes Laertius (c.250 CE) is said to have lived to 100. Pythagoras, who died around 405 BC, is credited with 70 or 80 years, and in the ancient

Greek and Roman world 'ancients' were not uncommon. Plutarch was 80 and Plato was 82 when they died. There is ample evidence of people living into their eighties and nineties in more recent historical times.[2] Bertrand Russell lived to 98. The difference is that now there are more and more of us living well beyond the average statistic.

So when is someone old? Is 50 the magic number? Is 70 the new 60? Are we old when we qualify for a Seniors Card? When we retire from the workforce? When we qualify for the pension? When we get sick? When we have grandchildren? When we get grey hair? When we access our superannuation? These points are arbitrary but all describe a boundary from which there is no return. Once we are defined as 'old' we are assigned to a category. We are often patronised, ignored, shouted at, called *love*, *dear* and *darling*—instead of our names—and expected to dwell on the margins of society.

Donald Hall, a writer for the *New Yorker* (and friend of Henry Moore, the sculptor), recently described an incident when, after exiting a museum cafeteria, he stopped to admire a Moore carving from his wheelchair. He was approached by a guard, who bent over to address him. 'The guard wagged a finger in my face, smiled a grotesque smile, raised his voice and asked, "Did we have a nice din-din?"'[3] You can hear the condescension behind the words; visit any nursing home and you will hear the same tone.

Old age simply does not conjure up images of vital, active, interesting people; we think instead of people who are in need of care, physically disabled, and losing control of their bodily functions. We regularly see images of such people in popular media, often looking almost extraterrestrial.

While the ageing Baby Boomers are challenging the stereotype, and the market is registering opportunity (because Boomers do have money to spend), even they are stigmatised by images and stories depicting them as indulgent 'younger oldies'. Boomers are described as gallivanting around the country in caravans on one long holiday, eroding their children's futures by draining their superannuation funds.[4] Questions are also raised about whether they will live up to their responsibilities and care for the 'extreme oldies'—their parents—who are already 'burdening' the state. Both groups—the Boomers in their fifties and sixties and their parents in their eighties and nineties—are described as 'old': the Boomers are the burden of the future, while their parents are the current burden. As the journalist Kate Legge writes: 'It's the Baby Boomers' burden. With their parents living longer than ever, the weight of care is falling on a generation who may—or may not—step up...as [their parents] navigate their way into frailty.'[5]

This presents a far from accurate picture. Boomers *are* stepping up. They have been dubbed 'the sandwich generation' precisely because in their fifties and sixties they provide care in both directions: for their kids and their grandchildren, and often for their parents. They help their children buy homes or live longer in the family home because they can't afford to move out. They look after grandchildren, and are the biggest providers of informal childcare: one third of all children under 12 years old are cared for by grandparents. One in every five older people is the main carer for the disabled.[6]

This generation saved their money. Their parents, the subject of this book, lived through the Great Depression and World War Two; they understood rationing, they darned their socks and turned the lights off; they didn't carry credit cards. The stoicism they developed has not entirely escaped their Boomer children, who are now playing a responsible role in caring for their parents. For the first time in history they sit between three generations and they don't warrant the hyperbole of the selfish and indulgent generation. Such descriptions have helped create one of the myths that confuse the debate about ageing: that the burden of the aged may destroy the economy.

No one is sure what to call those who fall within the 50–100-year span. As 'old' is used so loosely, and society so reveres the image of youth, some people refuse to use the word at all; they don't even like 'ageing'. 'Elders', 'the third age', 'new stage beyond midlife', 'mature' and 'seniors' all get an airing but there is no universally accepted term. Among those I interviewed, Lesley Falloon, at 93 a poster girl for late adulthood, speaks about what she will do when she gets old. Mary Owen, at 92, thinks you get old when you allow others to make your decisions. Flora Noyce, at 91, says, 'I have always hoped to reach old age; I hope I get there. I think I must be old as I am older than almost everyone I know and people say, "Aren't you marvellous?"' So let's take a look at what being old really means.

Despite the sharp increase in life expectancy in the past 100 years, we are still caught up in the assumptions from the beginning of the twentieth century when males could expect to live to 55 and women to 59. Old age was that short period of time between when we stopped working and when we died, rarely long enough to become a burden for anybody but ourselves.

For many reasons, average life expectancy rose steadily across the twentieth century. Infant mortality dropped significantly; inoculation, refrigeration, sanitation and public education contributed to a safer environment with abundant food, good housing and improved health services; research led to new pharmaceuticals and medical knowledge which have helped prolong life and counter disease. A 65-year-old man today will likely live to his mid-eighties and women will come close to reaching 90. This expectation will vary across ethnic groups and social class (with Aboriginals particularly disadvantaged) but in all groups life expectancy is increasing.[7] To live these years well we need to be respected as individuals, have the ability to reinvent ourselves, our work and purpose, and have access to good medical advice.

The language we use, our cultural attitudes and media reporting should not continue to create and amplify social problems that can be solved simply and bring benefit to all of us.

CHAPTER 2

THE MYTH OF
THE AGED-CARE
BURDEN

WITH these dramatic changes to life expectancy we need to re-evaluate society's negative perception of ageing. We need a revolution in thinking about the role, status, and well-being of an age group who are now the fastest growing in society. It must involve the workplace, medical and aged-care systems and a challenge to the media.

THE HEALTH MYTH

THE Productivity Commission report, *Caring for Older Australians*, released in 2011, was an attempt to find innovative ways to restructure a complex, underfunded, neglected system of aged care which has grown like Topsy. The report's recommendations provide a blueprint for a system that would enable greater choice for older Australians, promoting independence, good health, quality care, flexibility and improved access to a wider range of community-based and residential services. It was welcomed as a first step by National Seniors Australia because of its philosophical basis.[1] This cautious optimism has been undermined by the government's decision in November 2012 to cap bonds for aged-care accommodation. Derek McMillan, the chief executive officer of Australian Unity Retirement Living, claims 'the result of this intervention will be lower quality, more homogeneous aged-care facilities located further from elderly people's own communities'.[2] If he is correct, the result will be the exact opposite of the Productivity Commission's recommendation for quality, diversity and flexibility in the choices to be offered older Australians. As he says, capping accommodation bonds that secure a place in an aged-care facility is an example of decision-making processes where expedient politics dictates how older Australians will live out their lives, and not informed policy.

The Productivity Commission estimates that by 2050 the number of people aged 85 and over in Australia will increase to 1.8 million, 5.1 per cent of people. The number of Australians living to 100 is growing by 8.5 per cent a year and by 2050 that number is expected to reach 78,000.[3] The international database on longevity has identified 4200 living Australians who are older than 100 years. Dr John McCormack, Senior Lecturer in Health Sciences at La Trobe University, maintains a list of the over 100s.[4] 'Now,' he says, 'you have to be 106 (for females) and 105 (for males) to be on the list because I can't keep up with them.'[5] Australia has one of the highest proportions of centenarians in the world, exceeded only by the US, Norway, the Italian island of Sardinia and the Japanese island of Okinawa. We are an old-ageing country.[6]

We should be celebrating living longer lives as one of the greatest achievements of our time. Instead, this increase in the world's ageing population is viewed with trepidation. Political economist Robert Reich sees it as 'a far bigger threat to the world economy than the Eurozone debt crisis, US unemployment and the Chinese slowdown combined...a problem unfolding like a slow-motion train wreck'.[7] This assessment is from an active 66-year-old who is still contributing to political and economic debate at the highest levels.

As health care for the aged is seen as the basis of Reich's impending social catastrophe it is a good place to start to test his claim. The point is not to bemoan future health costs but to ensure we keep people healthy longer. In this discussion we need to focus on 'health span' as well as life span.[8]

It makes personal, economic and social sense that

as we are living longer we each need to take care of ourselves, as best we can, so that we do not become a burden to ourselves, our families, the community and the health system over an extended period. This is our individual responsibility. We also have a right to expect the best possible quality of life and effective health care in our old age from a system we have contributed to all our working lives, especially in a nation such as Australia, which is enjoying unprecedented prosperity. It is wrong to cast the debate in polarised terms which do nothing to strengthen intergenerational sympathies.

Yes, we know that our bodies will go into decline and we will die of some failure or disease, but a neglected body will perish much sooner than one well cared for. Disease prevention is the optimal objective for living a successful long life.

I learned however, when I turned 70, that doctors were not so interested in seeing me. Three encounters with cancer between my husband and me have made us particularly vigilant about body maintenance. Soon after my birthday, when I was told by my doctor I would no longer be reminded officially to have a two-yearly pap smear, my eyebrows went up. 'It's okay,' said the GP. 'You can still come in if you wish, we just won't be notifying you anymore that a smear is due.'

Soon after that revelation I went to see my gastroenterologist to arrange for a five yearly colonoscopy. The procedure was completed, there were no problems and, as I was leaving, my doctor said, 'You don't need to come back again.'

'You mean, ever?' I enquired.

'Yes,' he replied.

'But my father had bowel cancer in his mid-seventies, that's why I come in for regular check-ups,' I countered.

'Okay,' he said, 'you can come back.'

A few months later I had my annual mammogram, and my consulting specialist of 20 years' standing said, 'You're cancer-free after all this time, so you don't need to come back again.' Having served ten years as Chair of the Breast Cancer Network of Australia I am familiar with the statistics. I know that a woman's risk of breast cancer increases with age, and that if you have had breast cancer before—as I had 25 years ago—your risk is higher. My physician knew better than I that mutations in cancer genes accumulate with ageing. So I pressed him to explain what he was talking about.

It evolved that he was retiring and wouldn't be working a year from now. 'What are you doing with all your records?' I asked.

'I haven't thought about that,' he replied. 'I'll probably put them under the house.'

'What about giving them to your patients?' I suggested.

'I'll think about that,' was the response. But I knew from his lack of interest that earwigs and silverfish would win the day and my health records of more than

20 years, along with countless others, were destined to rot.

A little checking among my peers indicated that my experience of turning 70 was not unique. Several of my friends had been given the same message by their doctors: enough for me to conclude that the medical system wants to cull those over 70 from the groups receiving regular 'expensive' procedures because the expenditure is no longer considered cost-effective.[9]

I put this question to my GP, who explained tactfully that life-expectancy statistics do cut in about the time it would take a new cancer to develop. So if a person is cancer-free at 70 they will likely live to 78 or 82 (the current life-expectancy targets) if they get a new cancer. And as cancer is a disease of old age many will certainly contract it. My GP effectively confirmed that we are deemed by the medical profession, unofficially at least, to have lived our expected life span, and if cancer or anything else catches up with us, then that's too bad. Yet, an increasing number of 70-year-olds today remain active, defying current medical assumptions, with potentially the longest stage of their lives still ahead of them to continue to contribute to society.

At 76 my life is far from circumscribed. I write, I publish, I engage; I support and see my family, grandchildren and friends regularly; I read, I watch movies, television and theatre, walk, drive and go to the gym; I chair an international foundation, I sit on a theatre board, I act as a mentor to a number of people and get called on for advice; I travel widely, enjoy new experiences, organise two homes, engage with the community and take an interest in politics. I enjoy the new freedom from past responsibilities, and the ability to decide what I will do and when I will do it. I enjoy my life with my husband of 54 years. I don't cause trouble and I help out where I can. Yes, the years have taken some toll: I have arthritis and a successful hip replacement. Society may wish to define me as past my prime but I can see plenty of life to be lived yet. My lifelong friends are just as active and some are still working full-time at 75. Yet just at the time we can expand our horizons, insurance companies raise the cost of travel insurance and disallow multiple-trip policies in a 12-month period to people over the age of 75, on the grounds that they are too great a health risk. Beyond 80, travel insurance coverage is almost impossible to acquire, no matter how healthy you may be.

The myth that health costs and aged care will be the straws that break our system's back derives from simplistic analysis. The longer we work the more these costs will be relieved. Experts who look beyond the bottom line to examine the system point out that there are many ways it can become more cost-effective. Medical policy designed to marginalise the 'old' at 70 is not one of them. Effective health-care prevention programs before the age of 70 have increased the period of life that is free from disability and disease. Logic and sound social and economic planning suggest that since our life span will continue to increase it would make sense to continue to narrow the gap between health, ill health, decline and death and increase quality of life as long as possible. Disease prevention in the final decades of life would be a sounder policy than risking the cost of lengthy morbidity through turning a medical blind eye. The older you are the healthier you have been and those who live longer healthy lives can reasonably expect to have a short period of acute illness before they die.

For some years the media have pushed the Robert Reich narrative of the impending doom caused by an ever older, ever sicker population.[10] But living longer is far from the only factor contributing to higher medical costs.

Gary Banks, Chairman of the Productivity Commission, stated in June 2008: 'Ageing alone is estimated to push up health expenditure from $170 billion to $210 billion by 2045, an increase of 25 per cent. As a proportion of GDP, the increase is from 8.1 per cent to 10.3 per cent... to put that in perspective, Canada, Switzerland, France, Germany and the United States already have reached this level of health expenditure.'[11]

So it would seem that our expenditure on health services is not unreasonable for a developed country. As well, studies of *actual* health costs show that ageing is a *minor* part of cost increases in the medical process in Australia and internationally, and there are many significant ways in which costs can be reduced.

As part of a re-evaluation of ageing policies, medical guidelines for the dying must be improved. Many of us would like to plan the way we die, retain control and go without pain and trauma. As the Roman Stoic Seneca put it, 'The wise man will live as long as he ought not as long as he can.'[12] The idea of drawing up an advanced care plan which is signed, witnessed and accessible is becoming more common, but we are still not very good at talking about death. 'I'm not afraid of dying,' Woody Allen joked, 'but I don't want to be around when it happens.' In the absence of such talk, millions of dollars are wasted on 'futile' aggressive medical interventions for patients unable to speak for themselves and whose death is inevitable. It has been calculated that advanced care planning would save $250 million annually, not to mention avoiding the trauma of last-ditch efforts to extend the lives of patients. This is one burden on overstretched hospitals that could be eased.[13]

There has been a sharp increase in expenditure on technology, therapeutic appliances and pharmaceuticals since the late 1990s. These initiatives have some benefits and some downsides. It is argued that the exploding costs from the use and abuse of pharmaceuticals will be a major factor in undermining the Pharmaceutical Benefit Scheme (PBS) that progressive governments have put in place in Australia. For example, drugs to lower cholesterol (statins) are prescribed for two million Australians at a cost of more than a billion dollars. Yet the Director of the Baker IDI Heart and Diabetes Institute, Garry Jennings, has said, 'a University of Sydney study suggests the benefits of taking statins could outweigh the costs for a larger number of Australians'.[14]

The approval process for listing drugs on the PBS is complex. The underlying principle of the current subsidy is for the Pharmaceutical Benefits Advisory Committee (PBAC) to establish reasonable cost-effectiveness and make a recommendation to the Minister for Health about listing. Once a drug is recommended for approval, a separate arm of the Department of Health and Ageing—the Pharmaceutical Benefits Pricing Authority—negotiates the price and then the Minister approves the listing. If the total cost to government is more than $10 million per year the decision for approval goes to Cabinet. Around the world the standard model for cost-effectiveness is cost per quality adjusted life year (QALY) or life year gained (LYG). This allows drugs for patients with different diseases to be compared using one cost-effectiveness measure. At this time the threshold varies but a maximum of $50,000 per QALY is accepted in Australia, Canada and the UK. Unfortunately, once a drug is listed it can be difficult to renegotiate price. So at the moment, in general, the initial price remains the same until the patent for the drug expires and generic versions are produced at a lower price.

The system has come under scrutiny and criticism with the release of a report from the Grattan Institute[15] which argues that the federal government could save $1.3 billion each year by reforming the PBS and setting the same price for drugs that many Australian public hospitals or New Zealand's national pharmaceuticals purchasers pay. If the Australian government also encouraged doctors and patients to replace some drugs with others that achieve a similar result, at least another $550 million could be saved each year. The differences in prices paid for drugs by different states are also dramatic. The report argues that the pharmaceutical industry has far too much power in the pricing process and the government is reluctant to take on the industry. The current five-year deal with the pharmaceutical-manufacturing lobby group, Medicines Australia, expires in 2014 and there is an opportunity for reform. This should include reviewing any extensions to the life of drug patents, which expire later in Australia than in other countries. There are billions of dollars in potential savings at stake.

Advances in pharmaceuticals have reduced the need for treatment in hospitals and allowed the aged to remain in their homes, thereby reducing aged-care costs overall. But pharmaceutical companies are reaping a bonanza in profits from the PBS as more people seek access to drugs to help maintain well-being. In a process called 'ever-greening', a drug company will often apply for a new patent for a different form or application of a drug so that a generic copy cannot be made in competition. But companies producing generic drugs also have a vested interest in keeping costs high. The cost of drugs to the medical system must be monitored to determine appropriate usage, and renegotiated when necessary to achieve a sustainable balance. The drug companies should be able to achieve reasonable profits without exploiting the maintenance of a necessary system.

And then there is the new science of pharmaco-genomics. The Executive Director of the Australian Centre for Health Research, Neil Batt, claims the new science of prescribing drugs based on an individual's biomarkers, which can be examined through a simple blood test, is able to tell a doctor whether a patient will have a good response, a poor response or no response at all to a drug. Applying this science would save the health system $12 billion over the next five years from avoided adverse drug reactions and unnecessary pharmaceutical spending, as well as improve dramatically the lives of many patients, yet this is not happening.[16] Many health-care experts also believe it is inevitable that their industry will soon be transformed by a new model of care called 'precision medicine', based on digital and molecular models of an individual's genes, proteins, microbial communities and other sources of information. This will make preventive care much more effective.[17]

New technologies have already helped reduce rates

of hospitalisation and duration of hospital stays. Two examples of such advances are the use of improved anaesthetics for older patients and improved cataract surgery techniques. Doctors are calling for new surgical techniques to be subjected to the same level of scrutiny as new drugs.[18] Some doctors question the value of procedures such as arthroscopy, spine fusion of the lower back, and carotid artery surgery for people with blockages in the neck. There is mounting evidence they are ineffective and that other treatments could be more useful. A debate about redesigning health strategies would be more constructive and socially desirable for all than beating the drum about the impending financial burden. To this end, TEDMED—a multi-disciplinary community of innovators and leaders who share a common determination to create a better future in health and medicine—met in April 2013 in Washington DC. The conference called for radical innovation to solve the biggest global challenges in health, including diseases associated with ageing.

Michael D. Coory argues in the *Medical Journal of Australia* that promotion of the aged-care burden myth may have a political purpose:

> Population ageing has been used to justify current and popular ideological positions that favour the private health sector and seek to contain public sector activity. It has also distracted attention from the need to evaluate current patterns of care...

there is no evidence that population ageing will cause chaos throughout the health system. Policy-making in Australia would be improved if this was more widely acknowledged.[19]

Government has been successful in identifying areas for cost-effective reform in health: the HIV/AIDS campaign; the anti-smoking campaign; fluoridation of water; regulation of safety belts; and drink-driving campaigns. But we can do more. It is said that if doctors washed their hands regularly, $1 billion would be saved annually.[20] There should be a national program to advance health and well-being through consumer education, including exercise campaigns and programs aimed at protecting our cardiovascular, skeletal and muscular systems. Almost one-third of Australians over 65 do not exercise at all and injuries from falls among the elderly are increasing. We all have a responsibility to take care of ourselves and keep fit: the way we live will determine how long we live and how we die.[21] And the evidence is mounting that aerobic and resistance training can not only stem memory loss but also improve memory.[22]

Dementia is now seen as another 'looming burden'. The estimated current dementia prevalence globally is 35 million and this is expected to double every 20 years. Enormous effort is going into pharmaceutical solutions but interesting research reveals there may be simpler ways to lessen the 'burden'. Social isolation is believed to exacerbate dementia. A 2008 report by the Victorian Government showed there were more than 50,000 socially isolated Victorians over the age of 65 and this number is expected to increase to 75,000 by 2020.[23] The National Centre for Cognitive Decline is implementing new ways of dealing with dementia 'by treating the person as a person'.[24] New technologies may help counter isolation. Researchers are working on projects that aim to keep older people more connected through social media platforms so they can continue to make a valuable contribution. A study has shown a 45 per cent decrease in dementia among older people who regularly use a computer compared with those who don't.[25] Melbourne University's Institute for a Broadband-Enabled Society is investigating the use of mobile and broadband technologies to alleviate social isolation in older people. We need to develop courses on IT for 'oldies' for both their physical and mental well-being. This is hardly a radical approach.

If we implement what we know there will be massive savings, and it is important to recognise it is *more use* of the health system, not the ageing population, that has driven the bulk of the rise in health-care expenditure.[26]

If we compare the cost of ageing with the costs to society of obesity we can put the issue in better perspective. Monash University reports the prevalence of obesity in Australia has more than doubled in the past 20 years, with more than 17 million people ranked as overweight or obese—an extraordinary figure in a population of 23 million. The ABS estimates obesity costs Australia more than $58 billion per year.[27] This is a battle we are losing and it is an issue with serious ramifications for the health system. But obesity, despite claims from groups like the US National Association to Advance Fat Acceptance, is mostly self-inflicted and capable of solution in the same way as smoking is. These claims on the health system are society's burden, and not caused by old age.[28]

Old age is a natural and inevitable stage of life which has its particular needs, as do childhood, adolescence, adulthood and our working years. Those needs form part of our social contract with government, a key aspect of living in a democracy. The needs of old age should be seen as no more of a burden than childcare services, education services, gainful employment, health, disability and welfare services. At each stage of life the state provides essential services and does not scapegoat their recipients. The provisions for old age should be in the same category.

An enlightened approach to health reform could mean the extended years that medical science has given us can be put to a useful social and individual purpose. We are healthier than ever; we are much wealthier on average than any previous generation; we have paid our health insurance over the years; we have been active contributors to society throughout our lives and we will cost society less the more we look after ourselves. Significantly, we are better informed about health-care options and politically much more influential than the aged have been before us. And we are capable of continuing to contribute productively to our own upkeep as we always have. Only neglect and ignorance turn us into a burden.

THE PRODUCTIVITY MYTH

ROBERT Reich's rhetoric about inevitable decrepitude spills over from health care into the workplace. 'Beware the seniors,' the pundits cry.[29] Here, too, policy needs to catch up with reality. The discussion paper *Engaging and Retaining Older Workers*, released in March 2013 by the Australian Institute of Management, argues that increasing the participation of older workers will bring a double benefit: it will boost productivity and increase the supply of workers.[30] My aged peers should be welcomed to stay longer in the workforce so they can continue to support themselves and their valuable experience and expertise can be put to productive use.

There are at least three stereotypes about older workers that are not borne out by reality. The first is that they don't care about work anymore; the second is that they don't understand technology, and the third is that they are not interested in promotion or career moves. In some cases this may be correct but these problems can exist in any age group in any job.

At 70 we are perfectly capable of learning new skills and continuing to play a valued role. Cato the Elder, a Roman politician and statesman, began to learn Greek at age 80. The modern press is beginning to recognise the similar capacities and achievements of our older citizens. Margaret Bowman, at 91, won a creative fellowship at the State Library of Victoria to research the nineteenth-century artist George Alexander Gilbert.[31] Emeritus Professor Nancy Millis, a pioneer in biotechnology, drove daily from her home in Brighton to Melbourne University to work in the Department of Microbiology and Immunology for a full day's work until she was 90, when she died following a car accident.[32] Anna Schwartz, whose research became a classic study of the Great Depression, continued working until shortly before her death at 96. In a full and influential career she found time to bring up four children.[33] Jacques Barzun, the famous historian, published *From Dawn to Decadence: 500 years of Western cultural life, 1500 to the present* in his 94th year. He died at 104 and as a centenarian rose at 6am, exercised for 40 minutes and started his day's reading. He enjoyed cocktails before his evening meal.[34] A great example of a productive old age is Emeritus Professor Henry Atkinson, a former surgeon, academic and historian who continues to work one day a week at Melbourne University's dental museum as an honorary curator. He has no plans to retire and believes in remaining socially and intellectually stimulated.[35] Stanford University, where I studied film in the late 1960s, celebrated in 2013 the Class of '33, who graduated 80 years earlier. An invitation went to Ephraim Engleman, who at 102 is Director of the Rosalind Russell Medical Research Center for Arthritis. Engleman works three days a week administering the program he founded 34 years ago. He is as vigorous and healthy as most people 20 years younger and 'retirement is not an option.'[36] Such people are no longer rare; they are in the vanguard of a large group who will follow.

W. Somerset Maugham wrote, 'Old age is ready to undertake tasks that youth shirked because they would take too long.'[37] People must continue to work, and many want to work—not just for the good of the economy but for their own well-being—and the medical system needs to be structured to support their healthy longevity.

Unfortunately, like Robert Reich, the Treasury in Australia seems obsessed with the costs of an ageing society: it has been the theme of its three intergenerational reports over the past decade. Treasury concludes that the accommodation and care costs of the aged will squeeze a fortune from future workers. But Treasury's narrow view is leading us up the garden path. Tim Colebatch describes the basis of the Treasury analysis as follows:

> In 2006 there were 14 million Australians aged 15 to 64, conventionally defined as working age, and

2.7 million over 65. The ratio of workers to retirees was 5.2 to 1. By 2056, on conservative assumptions, the Bureau projects that those of working age will grow by half, to 21.5 million, but the number of us 65 and over will treble to 8.1 million. The ratio of workers to retirees would then be 2.6 to 1. How could tomorrow's workers be expected to finance so many retirees, especially when those aged 85 and over, with the most chronic needs for care, are projected to increase from 322,000 to 1.72 million?[38]

What Colebatch fails to point out is that economists (including those in Treasury) use an arbitrary definition of the 'dependency ratio': the number of non-working dependants as a proportion of the number of productive workers. It's a flawed formula of infinite flexibility, depending on the assumptions you build into it. A lower birth rate means fewer dependent children and youth, lower costs for maternity hospitals, child-care benefits and schools. An increase in productivity, through advanced technology or improved management systems, of a mere 0.5 per cent would cover the costs of aged-care and aged-health expansion. Bringing in skilled migrants may boost productivity but, since they are likely to be young, will also swell the numbers of families with dependent children. And what is dependency anyway, when we know the flows of both financial assistance and moral support run from old to young more than from young to old?[39]

What, even, is productivity when the GDP fails to measure the significant dollar-value of caring work, voluntary work, community work and creative work, without which our economy could not function, and none of which is a monopoly of the young? Those over 55 contribute the staggering sum of $74.5 billion a year through caring for spouses and grandchildren and in other unpaid voluntary work. Women aged 65 to 74 contributed $16 billion in unpaid work inside and outside the home; men of that age, who are fewer in number, contributed another $10.3 billion.[40]

The Australian Bureau of Statistics measures GDP four times a year—it is considered that important—yet a survey of 'time-use' has not been conducted since 2006. To save funds the Bureau cancelled its long-scheduled Work Life and Family Survey in 2013 and there won't be another until 2019. This survey would have told us how much time women are spending in paid and unpaid work, including caring for kids; how much work is done by volunteers; how much time is spent caring for invalids and the frail; how women's participation in the paid workforce is changing as they become better educated. But this information, which is critical for understanding social well-being, is being given no priority. A government can't manage what it does not know and it can't know what it refuses to measure.[41]

In Treasury's analysis the first assumption to be challenged is that older people will not work after the age of 65 and that the costs of medical care, aged care, pensions, concessions and tax-free superannuation will all escalate. As we have seen, Baby Boomers can expect to live to 90, so 65 is far too early for retirement and the trend is already for people to stay in work longer. A decade or two ago, early retirement was a widely held ambition—touted as 'the golden years', a time for a well-deserved rest, playing some golf and travelling—but there has been a massive cultural shift. Full-time leisure is not as enticing as it first seems, and the Global Financial Crisis (GFC) and loss of superannuation funds prompted a change of heart for many. Early retirement looks more like unemployment.

Prior to the GFC most women had retired by their late fifties and only one in five went on working past 60. Today 43 per cent of women in their early sixties, and 17 per cent in their late sixties, are still working. And it is not only women staying at work in record numbers; more than one in four Australians aged 65–69 are working, most of them full time, and there are now more workers over 55 than under 25.[42] According to the Australian Bureau of Statistics, in 2011, 102,000 people (7.5 per cent) were working in their seventies, eighties and nineties—up from 59,000 a decade ago—and this revolution in the workforce is rolling on.[43] ABS data shows only 13 per cent of workers plan to retire by 60, with those planning to retire at 65 or later rising from 47 per cent to 58 per cent. Those who say they will never retire have gone from 384,000 to 575,000. Australia is still far behind world leaders, particularly Iceland, where 81 per cent of people aged 55 to 64 work, but we are on the move and economic gains from this cultural shift will change the gloomy predictions which dominate the debate about ageing and the economy.[44]

A discussion paper aimed at removing barriers to older people finding work and staying in the workforce was released by the Australian Law Reform Commission in October 2012. It recommends a suite of proposals, including that the retirement age for judges and the military be lifted, that volunteer workers be entitled to workers' compensation for injury on the job and that workers be able to contribute to superannuation over the age of 75. The current limit is an impediment to those planning their financial security.[45] These are moves in the right direction with employers required since June 2013 to make superannuation payments to those 70 years and older.

It isn't easy to find a job at a mature age and in difficult economic times, but people generally, especially women, are staying in employment longer and not just for economic reasons.[46] Having a purpose in life is central to health and well-being, and work often provides that purpose: this does not change with age. Psychologists have found that people generally report as their happiest moments the times when they were working hard at something, moving towards a goal, being challenged, absorbed and focused, rather than when they were lying on the beach or going to parties.[47]

A government looking beyond the next election could alleviate these economic pressures by lifting the age that people can access super funds at low tax rates above 55 years; rolling back the age when superannuation can be taken tax-free to 65; speeding up the move to a higher pension age with concessions to 70. We need to promote a culture in which working to 70 and beyond is seen as normal. We must tackle the enduring, endemic ageism of corporate human relations managers for this to work, and, to this end, there is now some evidence that, apart from the consideration of individual satisfaction and quality of life, the economy can be sufficiently stimulated in the long term only if Australian employers hire more older workers.[48]

In 1999, a Drake survey of 500 HR managers reported that not one would employ someone over 50, and 65 per cent would prefer to retrench those over 45 rather than anyone younger, regardless of their skills and performance. Recently I heard a story from an HR manager attending a meeting about how to terminate employees and on what grounds. They were discussing a case study of a long-serving 59-year-old employee who was having trouble meeting deadlines. 'Get rid of her,' was the unanimous response from the younger people present.

I admit with some shame that I too was guilty of

such thinking when employing staff as Director of the Australian Children's Television Foundation. I believed the energy, drive, innovative thinking and commitment I was looking for would not be found in older employees. I stepped down when I was 65 and later I heard it had been said I had stayed too long in the job. I would do things differently today and that reflects the significant change in attitudes over the past decade. I talked with a number of CEOs about their experience of stepping down and discovered that this practice of the heir apparent belittling the past incumbent is not uncommon. It possibly relates to the way politics is played out in Australia, but I feel sure that ageism is a contributing factor and an attitude we need to combat as we encourage older workers to remain in the workforce.

Employers are slowly realising that the old are more reliable, more productive and more costly to replace with inexperienced younger workers. This, too, is a significant culture shift. This is about late adults benefiting from a life in a society they have helped create. Economists have too narrow a definition of productivity, which is not useful in evaluating either a 'good' life or the functions that need to be filled in our modern society. Excluding the value of voluntary work, of holding a family together, of caring for others, of keeping life ticking along while others work in paid employment ignores these roles which act as the glue that binds a community.

CHAPTER 3

MINDFUL PURPOSE

BEING healthy and being productive are in fact two sides of the one coin in leading a purposeful and engaging life. It's not just a job that gives meaning; it's having the capacity to live life as we choose. Health care is not the only or even the major concern for many individuals who are now living beyond their nineties. Learning how to live mindfully, with a purpose that makes us want to get out of bed in the morning, is the most important priority if we are to transform the last stage of life. We fear boredom almost as much as death. The relevant issue for the medical system in this context will be managing the psychosocial aspects of individual lives: that is, the way people see themselves and are seen in their community. To achieve success here will mean questioning deep-rooted attitudes.

My father and mother did not, by example, prepare me for the tribulations of old age. They were fit and active people who lived at home together in the country town of Mildura until my mother died two weeks after a stroke just after my 60th birthday. My father lived alone for another two years and despite some memory loss he resisted any attempt to move him into a facility where he would have had company and care. He lived contentedly until he put himself to bed one night, fully clothed, and left the heater on. There was a 40 degree heat wave in Mildura and Reg was not discovered for two days, by which time he was severely dehydrated. He was hospitalised and the doctor was unsure he would recover, so he was placed in nursing-home care. But at 94 he was still resilient and gradually he did recover. He then actually enjoyed his life in a nursing home at Red Cliffs, where most of the residents had gone to die. But things soon went wrong. After a while the matron wanted him moved out because she could get more money for a bed with a more disabled person than my father. She also asserted that he was a troublemaker.

Reg shared a room with a man with no legs, who couldn't get out of bed but used to turn the television up very loud. My father had macular disease, so couldn't see the television, didn't like the noise, and would leave his bed to pull the plug out of the wall socket. There were simple solutions to the problem—giving the television-viewer earphones or putting the two men in different rooms—but they seemed to be beyond the wit of the administration. I made it very clear that my father would not be moved out of the nursing home without a public argument. The matron backed off, separated the two men and my father settled down again.

Then Reg got shingles; he slipped on a polished floor, fell and broke his hip. How often do we hear this story about an elder? The hip mended, but Reg could not relearn how to move his legs so that he could walk again. He was 95 years old, he had lost his lifelong partner, and although he had no heart disease, cancer or identified illness—terminal or otherwise—this was the final straw. He had had enough: he had lost his interest in living. Where he lived provided him with his physical needs, food and accommodation, but no purpose.

I travelled to Mildura, along with my daughter, to see my dad, and we took him in his wheelchair to a park. Then we bought some fish and chips, which he usually enjoyed, and we sat eating on a balcony outside his room. He was sucking on a chip when I asked, 'Dad, what are you thinking about?'

'I'm thinking about the good time I'd be having if I was having a good time,' was the response: one he would have given in his prime. It was so typical of him. He asked to be helped onto his bed and he never got up again. He died less than a week later on 3 September 2000 and joined my mother in a carefully chosen cemetery plot.

Apart from a breakdown early in his life from overwork, and bowel cancer in his mid-seventies, he had had few illnesses. He would not go to the doctor, and on three occasions when forced by his family into hospital—for surgery after a gall bladder attack, the removal of a lump on his neck, and proposed prostate surgery after dehydration—he discharged himself and refused treatment. On each of those three occasions his symptoms disappeared. His hair greyed but not completely. At 95 he looked younger than much younger men. He had been a pioneer in a remote Australian town and he retained the spirit and tenacity of one who had learned to rely on himself. In his late years the major issue for my father, who had been a significant force in public life over seven decades, was remaining relevant and finding a purpose in a community all too eager to discard the experience and skills he had learned over a long life.

My parents were never a burden on the health system. Their lives highlight some of the issues elders must now deal with to retain dignity, especially once they enter a care facility. Nursing homes and care facilities generally give token regard to intellectual stimulation for their residents. Muriel Crabtree, a vital independent woman, who, at 102 years of age, was forced to go into a care facility following a fall, was denied her occupation: she was not permitted to draw with her 'dusty' pastels. She had become a competent artist and drawing had been her absorbing interest for more than three decades after her retirement from Melbourne University. For reasons of 'tidiness' Muriel was not permitted to draw in her room and was told there was nowhere else in the building she could go. Without any purpose other than getting through the day, she lost her interest in living. It is a cruel reality that care in late adulthood often takes little account of an individual's social and psychological needs.

This failure to understand and encourage an individual's passion is born of the assumption that unpaid leisure activities have no 'serious' status and can be substituted for something else; people are expected simply to fill in their time. In institutions, seating residents in front of a television set often seems to suffice as an adequate time-filler; it's what we used to do with our children. But the same principle applies at both ends of life: the brain requires more than diversion. Children who spend excessive hours in front of television are disadvantaged intellectually and emotionally; adults are too. They require a diverse range of activities for stimulation: interesting conversation and debate is essential. Speakers and discussions; craft classes; games like chess, Scrabble and cards; crosswords; book clubs; film groups; learning how to use the computer, mobile phones and tablets; relationships with young people through links with schools: all these activities can be scheduled in care facilities. Providing stimulation is as essential for any care program as providing meals. Unless a person is demented they can continue to function as they have all their lives. They do not lose their wits when they cease work unless they are ignored and neglected. And those of us with dementia benefit from social and intellectual stimulation.

Despite the fact that internet usage is becoming ubiquitous with the under sixties its use remains patchy for older Australians. There is a socioeconomic divide with internet usage but also an age divide. Two-thirds of households headed by people over 80 do not have access to the internet. These people may not be predisposed to use computers because of lack of experience but they should be encouraged to learn, in beginners classes for seniors. Every aged community should have such a program and all retirement homes should have multiple points of internet access. This group presents a huge opportunity commercially but, more importantly, their old age could be transformed by the myriad uses a computer provides. It is a tool as important as the telephone for earlier generations, enabling people to connect with others and form personal and interest-based relationships. Computer usage can alleviate isolation and bring family and friends closer, and some individuals may even find part-time work via the internet.[1] I was 65 when I began to use the computer and could not even manipulate a mouse. I called on my children and grandchildren for technical assistance often, and still do. Using technology is a great way to connect with grandchildren and peers. This poem, which captures the technology gap, was sent to me by Jim Brierley.

The computer swallowed Grandma,
Yes, honestly it's true!
She pressed 'control' and 'enter'
And disappeared from view.
It devoured her completely,
The thought just makes me squirm.
She must have caught a virus
Or been eaten by a worm.
I've searched through the recycle bin
And files of every kind;
I've even used the Internet,
But nothing did I find.
In desperation, I asked Mr Google
My searches to refine.
The reply from him was negative,
Not a thing was found 'online'.
So, if inside your 'Inbox',
My Grandma you should see,
Please 'Copy', 'Scan' and 'Paste' her,
And send her back to me.

This poem was written as a tribute to all the
Grandmas & Grandpas who have learned to use
the Computer...
We do not stop playing because we grow old;
We grow old because we stop playing...

As we age we must prepare for lifelong activities which give us a purpose. Abolishing compulsory retirement has been a positive step forward in recognising the need for people to remain active. But pressure is still applied to workers to move out of jobs as they age, despite evidence of older people performing well in responsible roles. History records more than a few examples. Winston Churchill was elected prime minister of the UK at the age of 77 and served until he was 81; Charles de Gaulle, thought to be the greatest French statesman, served his final term as president when he was 75, resigning at 79. Konrad Adenauer, who was chancellor of West Germany, was elected at 73 and held the position for 14 years. Ronald Reagan was 74 when re-elected US president, and the reigning emperor of Japan is 79.

Those who have enjoyed their working years know how astonishing is the energy you can find when you are deeply engaged with what you are doing. I was often asked, 'How do you manage to do what you do?' In my case my work was energising. I could become exhausted doing little, but bounce back every day to do work I loved. Both former US secretary of state Hillary Clinton and Australia's Governor-General, Quentin Bryce, have responded similarly when asked about the way they cope with their demanding roles.

This is not necessarily the case for those who have earned their living through physical labour, so retirement policies must be flexible enough to take account of an individual's physical well-being. But no matter what the circumstances, retirement is a dramatic and often traumatic change in a person's life, altering the way they see themselves, and we do not give enough thought and preparation to this major transition. Many elders struggle with grief, depression and questions of identity when they retire. Geriatricians describe this phenomenon as a loss of 'generativity', when at the end of a productive life people experience an identity crisis: they panic when they are faced with a blank diary, and regret lost opportunities.[2] They feel people regard them differently.

John Banville describes this loss in his novel, *Ancient Light*:

> It must be hard to get used to there being nothing urgent that needs to be done...Theirs I imagine is a world without impetus. I see them envying the busyness of others, eyeing resentfully the lucky postman on his round, the housewives with their shopping baskets, the white-coated men in vans delivering necessary things. They are the unintended idlers, the ones astray, the at-a-loss ones.[3]

Retirement needs careful planning. It is not the time to cut all ties and head off to live in a warm climate, but rather to ask: Who do I want to be near? How will my relationships be reaffirmed? What do I care about? What can I create and contribute to the world? It is through these questions that we will find meaning in our new life.

When I retired from the workforce, I had to drive my own routine. I missed the obligations that motivated me to work on many levels; the social contacts work provided, like them or not; the adrenaline rush and the satisfaction of completing a challenging task. I missed the excitement of coming up with a good idea and carrying it through. I felt ambivalent about leaving the Australian Children's Television Foundation after so many years of leading the debate about children and media. But it was the choice I made. I wanted to continue to work so I had to learn new skills—particularly computer skills, as I planned to write—and do all the things I had delegated to others. I had to learn to deal with answering systems that never supplied the information I was looking for, manage my own bookings, appointments, banking. And I did, laboriously. Necessity is indeed the mother of invention.

I kept busy and at first did not comprehend that I was entering possibly the longest stage of my life. My childhood, adolescence, first career, married life with children, second and third careers, kids moving out of home, grandchildren arriving and 20 years as Director of the ACTF (which was the longest period of time I had worked continuously in one place) were behind me. Only married life with the one partner for 53 years provided continuity for the years ahead. I didn't think about ageing. But suddenly I was faced with a new freedom as there was no imperative to do anything other than what I felt like doing. It was a shock. Once I completed the tasks I had lined up, and done my share of relaxing, I had to think about what I would do next. This had never happened before; one thing had always led to another. Full-time leisure had no appeal but now nobody really cared if I did nothing. Still, it was not in my nature to plan on sitting in a chair for the next 20 years or so, nursing my ailments. This is one reason I came to write this book. I became fascinated with old age, watching and talking to people older than myself, people who have continued to pursue interesting lives and have continued to find purpose. What was their secret?

CHAPTER 4

SELF-BELIEF

SUCCESSFUL elders maintain belief in themselves and remain motivated to contribute to society. It is not easy to do this if they see no evidence that they are valued as individuals, and for the old this is often the case. The bad press the elderly receive is evidence of pervasive ageism and its effects are as sinister as racism or sexism. Ageism differs in that it is not directed at a minority group; it impacts on men and women of every race. Only those who die young will escape the stigma. But the predominant images of old age are out of keeping with the evidence. Most people don't think about ageing until it is upon them and then fight its progression in denial for years. We don't want to be cast on the scrapheap, lose our status and identity or fit into a stereotype.

Western society glorifies youth and we are all

susceptible to media propaganda about appearance. I attempted to delay ageing by grooming. Working in male-dominated professional businesses, first in a university and then the media industry, I dressed with some flair. In 1974, with Hilary McPhee, I wrote a book called *Media She*, in which we railed against the pressures imposed on women about their appearance.[1] We have made progress on many fronts, but the pressure to look younger than we are and to measure up to a standard of desirable beauty bordering on perfection has not changed. A successful woman must be thin, unwrinkled, have even white teeth and shoulder-length hair, and, in this age of 'the celebrity', fit a surprisingly cloned air-brushed image.

The market has traded on our fear of looking old with the development of body industries worth billions to the economy as women and men dye their hair, moisturise skin, shave hair from all parts of their bodies, subject themselves to extreme body-building programs, endure plastic surgery from the vagina to the eyebrow and disguise wrinkles with botox injections and filler. Anti-ageing clinics are now building a broad clientele, administering supplements to counteract the ageing process.

But no matter how much we invest in anti-ageing treatments, the process is inexorable. It is 100 per cent certain we will age and we will die. We can control, to a limited extent, the speed of this process, but old age will take hold of us and when it does it comes as a surprise. If we are told we don't look our age we take it as a compliment. But finally we are forced to accept that we will lose the fight to look young and we will join the ranks of the invisible aged. We catch an unexpected view of ourselves in a window and think, *That can't be me.*

The fight the aged must take on has similarities to the feminist movement of the 1970s. Back in 1973 prime minister Gough Whitlam made a speech about injustice towards women: 'the first and fundamental step towards freedom is awareness by women themselves of their real inequality, the extent of social, political, economic and cultural discrimination and deprivation.'[2] A host of feminist writers and activists agreed and government responded by enacting policies outlawing gender discrimination. We no longer live as they do in *Mad Men* but feminism has not resolved the image issues women still face. So it is with the aged.

We have lacked strength in society, but the vote is a powerful weapon which can be used to demand better treatment and dignified debate. The response will be a measure of our society and civilisation.

First we must demand more from the media. Remember when there were no black people shown on television or, if there were, they were maids, labourers, singers or comics? I once worked in Chicago, in 1968, on a Ford Foundation Project placing teams of teachers into inner-city schools to help break down the power of the street gangs and lift the education levels of black students. One of my research colleagues, Yolande, told me her young son had asked her, 'Why don't I ever see myself on television?' As a black child his television option was to watch sitcoms such as *The Partridge Family*, *Leave it to Beaver*, *My Three Sons* and *I Dream of Jeannie* after school. Sidney Poitier had only just come to dinner in 1967. He was the perfectly credentialled black man, a handsome doctor who shocked the well-intentioned white liberal parents (Hepburn and Tracey) because he wanted to marry their daughter. It took some years and a civil rights movement before Morgan Freeman, Denzel Washington, Will Smith, Eddie Murphy, Whoopie Goldberg and Oprah became household names. Black women could get a public profile by singing, like Lena Horne, Josephine Baker, Dorothy Dandridge, Dionne Warwick, Whitney Houston and Beyoncé Knowles, but both white and black women have had their struggle to secure substantive and diverse roles beyond those of bombshell, whore, entertainer and domestic.

Nowadays the group most absent from the screen is the older generation. Research has shown that the more television you watch the more likely your attitude to the old will be negative.[3] As the old are rather heavy users of television, they will, like Yolande's boy, be absorbing the message that their lives are not important. The invisibility of old people on US television is striking and the clearest indication of how little they are valued. If the old are shown at all they are physically incapacitated or comic. Even the series *Grumpy Old Men* and *Grumpy Old Women* are based on a false premise. We do not become grumpier as we age.

The British are much better than the Americans at depicting a range of ages on screen, with regular roles for actors of such stature as Maggie Smith, Judi Dench and Helen Mirren (Meryl Streep is an American exception) but we rarely see a diversity of old people represented. Four recent films about ageing—*The Best Exotic Marigold Hotel*, *And If We All Lived Together*, Dustin Hoffman's directorial debut *Quartet*, and *Song of Marion*, starring Vanessa Redgrave and Terence Stamp—tackle the problems of continuing to 'live the dash' with humour and respect. *Amour*, directed by the Austrian Michael Haneke, which garnered the Oscar for best foreign film in 2013 and nominations for best picture, best director and best leading actress, portrays an octogenarian couple facing the end of their long and loving lives. *Still Mine*, with Geneviève Bujold and James Cromwell, tells another moving end-of-life story. There is a growing demand for these films. The very popular *Downton Abbey*, starring the redoubtable Maggie Smith, has a large audience, 35 per cent of whom are over 60 years old.

London's Royal Court Theatre has been a long-time supporter of new playwrights and the company is now turning its attention to an older age bracket, calling for first-time playwrights in their eighties to try their hand at the art form. A group of six to eight octogenarians will create short works that will then receive a staged reading and, should any pass muster, they will go on for further development.

Generally the aged provide a wealth of comic material on their looks, their capabilities (or lack thereof), their attitudes and their bodily functions, in stereotypes showing wrinkled, misshapen, frail, demented, drooling, rather repulsive creatures. They are often portrayed as impotent, toothless, deaf and flatulent. Such pervasive images rob the aged of self-esteem and contribute to a belief that they are deserving only of a place to rest out of sight, until death takes them.

A clever comedian can make satirical observations seem accurate and even the mundane very funny: think of Barry Humphries' creation, Sandy Stone. But a visit to a greeting-card shop will show how crude the stereotypes are. *Show me your tits*, reads the slogan on a young man's T-shirt as he stands at a bus stop; an old lady approaches with her shopping trolley, and lifts her coat to show her breasts hanging at knee level. A cartoon shows old Ethel reading out instructions to old Stanley, who is mounting a computer trying to set it up to use. Ethel's speech balloon says, 'Oops! Wait a minute honey; it says insert your floppy diSk!'

Jokes are now sent widely on the internet. I have a few friends with a regular supply, sending up the foibles we can relate to: they are amusing among ourselves. Deafness and farting are favourite topics. It is the ubiquitous nature of the message that makes depictions of the aged offensive. It is important we do not take ourselves too seriously and it is healthy to be able to laugh at oneself, but to be laughed at by others can be demeaning and degrading. Free speech should not be curtailed because someone may be offended, and when images are diverse, reflecting the infinite variety of individuals, then no one should be concerned. But when language, images and humour in common usage perpetually denigrate a group—the aged—it has a powerful effect.

In 2013 Council on the Ageing (Victoria) launched a campaign to bring Victoria international recognition as an age-friendly community, building on an initiative of the World Health Organization (WHO). The key factors making for a safe and enjoyable age-friendly community are access to good transport services, appropriate housing, civic participation, employment, supportive health services and respect for people. An age-friendly community promotes life opportunities and is inclusive.[4]

Reaching a century used to be a rare event but is now a growing phenomenon. People over 90 are the fastest growing population group in the country but we know very little about them. An ongoing study of more than 200 Sydney centenarians by the Centre for Healthy Brain Ageing at the University of New South Wales has found very positive characteristics generally. Centenarians' lifestyles share common traits, including not smoking or drinking excessively and maintaining a healthy weight throughout their lives. They are resilient, open to change and maintain good relationships. They are pretty good at coping with loss, and have low neuroticism, anger and hostility; they measure high on extroversion, openness and conscientiousness and their depression rate is low. They rate highly on trust, competence and dependability; they are easygoing and respond well to advice.[5] They also report lower levels of cardiac disease and diabetes than people in their eighties.[6] Centenarians tend to be independent, optimistic, cheerful and busy.[7]

While about 20 to 30 per cent of one's likelihood of living to 100 is determined by genes, and longevity does run in families, personality and attitude are just as important in determining whether we will live a long life. The Harvard Study of Adult Development, which began 75 years ago, is one of the most comprehensive examinations of ageing ever conducted.[8] Researchers have followed more than 800 men and women, from adolescence through to old age, seeking clues to the behaviours that translate into a happy and healthy later life. They have found: marriages after 70 in general get better; life at 80 for more than half the men was regarded as one of the happiest periods of their lives. While at 40 you worry about the neighbours, having a better car or whether you will have enough money for retirement, after 70 it just doesn't matter. A happy marriage at 50 predicts resilient healthy ageing at 80. Intellectual curiosity and lifelong learning are also important predictors of ageing well.

One of the most surprising findings was that stressful events don't predict future health and happiness. Old people who have had their share of trials and tribulations—experiencing war, famine, dislocation from their homeland and the loss of loved ones—were often happy and flourishing in their seventies and eighties. It is the way they dealt with trauma and tragedy that was critical to well-being. The study demonstrates 'that most people's lives are more authentically stories of growth and change than they are tales of demographic or genetic destiny'.[9] In fact, old people are a much more positive, competent group than the stereotypes suggest. Yet it is hard to change deep-seated assumptions and prejudice.

Scholars are now studying the places where people live longest in an effort to understand longevity. The Nuoro province in Sardinia, Italy, has the highest population of male centenarians in the world. The world's longest-lived women are found on the island of Okinawa. In 2008 a study began in Ikaria, in Greece, which concluded that people there were reaching the age of 90 at two and a half times the rate Americans were. 'Ikarian men in particular are nearly four times as likely as their American counterparts to reach 90, often in better health...and they suffered less depression and about a quarter the rate of dementia.'[10] Although they have no idea how the Ikarians got to be so old, researchers have identified 'subtly powerful, mutually enhancing and pervasive factors at work'. The people of Ikaria rest each afternoon, their food is healthy, natural and accessible—yoghurt and honey, a tasty stew of beans (lentils, chickpeas), seasonal vegetables (greens, pumpkin, potatoes, black-eyed peas, tomatoes, fennel), garlic and olive oil; bread, goat's milk and goat meat. They walk up and down hills every day, and contribute to the community, gardening, tending the animals and socialising. There is no crime, everyone knows everyone and their business, and they are never alone. At day's end they share a cup of seasonal herbal tea and drink several glasses of wine in the company of lifelong friends. There is an 'ecosystem' that makes ageing possible. And culture, belonging and purpose are very important parts of the mix.[11]

In the wider world, even in our advanced societies, such a supportive 'ecosystem' does not exist. Although Simone de Beauvoir wrote *The Coming of Age* over four decades ago, she makes clear why changing perceptions, even today, will be difficult.

> The most important fact to emphasise is that the status of the old man is never *won* but always *granted*...Their authority is based upon the dread or the respect they inspire: the moment the adults break free from this, the aged have no power left whatsoever...

It is the meaning that men attribute to their life; it is their entire system of values that define the meaning and the value of old age. The reverse applies: by the way in which a society behaves towards its old people it uncovers the naked, and often carefully hidden, truth about its real principles and aims.[12]

The aged now have more demographic and economic power than they had back then: they are better equipped to challenge the status quo and will do so, but social revolutions take time and the views the aged hold of themselves are far from homogeneous.

For example, Anthony Burgess, the author of *A Clockwork Orange*, was only 56 years old when he wrote in 1973:

As for myself, all I can say is that I am growing old, my sight is blurring, my teeth always need attention, I cannot eat or drink as much as I once did, I am more and more frequently bored. I cannot remember names, my reason works slowly, I have spasms of envy of the young and of resentment at my own imminent decay. If I had a burning faith in personal survival, this gloom of senescence might be greatly mitigated. But I have lost this faith and am unlikely to recover it. Sometimes I have a desire for immediate annihilation, but the urge to remain alive always supervenes. There are consolations—love, literature, music, the colourful life of the southern city in which I spend much of my time—but these are very fitful.[13]

Burgess was 76 when he died.

At 73, Colleen McCullough said of her life: 'Old age is an ordeal of flesh and mind. Of winding down, of dying cells. It's accepting the loss of physical attractiveness and replacing it with the power and the wisdom that only come with old age.'[14]

In his memoir *Winter Journal*, Paul Auster writes of ageing and death: 'Fouling the deathbed with piss and shit and drool. We are all going there...the question is to what degree a person can remain human while hanging on in a state of helplessness and degradation.'[15]

William Ian Miller (who calls himself an ageing professor although only 65) is another with a negative view of ageing. He has written a book called *Losing It* in which he laments his shrinking brain.[16] It is an erudite, blackly funny, curmudgeonly and pessimistic discourse—clever, but Miller's vision is not the experience of the long livers studied at Harvard or those in this book.

These writers depict dispiriting models for those anticipating a long old age. The cartoonist Michael Leunig is more philosophical and agreeable:

> The trick of good ripening is to keep the heart warm. This appears to be the great task of old-age and rather than closing the doors as we do in winter to keep the house warm, we must open

our hearts as wide as possible. That's what keeps you warm. Perhaps this is a lifetime's work and it is better to start earlier than later.[17]

Miriam Schmierer was Australia's oldest citizen when she died at 112; her life had spanned three centuries. When asked how she got there, she replied, 'Just quietly, living one day at a time'.[18] There is wisdom in that simple statement.

There is no question that attitude influences longevity, not only how long you live but the extent to which you enjoy your long life. Nature helps us because the brain develops over time and we learn to show better judgment as we age. We have experience to draw on to develop integrity and wisdom, which give us more perspective as we age. Old age is already slowly being transformed, but politically and socially we are struggling to identify what needs to be done to catch up with the reality of changes in life expectancy. There have always been old people; the difference now is not that the human life span has increased but that *more* people are living *much* longer and then dying much more quickly.

The old I am writing about, who have survived the trials of their long journeys, are steadily changing the perception of ageing. These elders generally have enjoyed fulfilling lives and there is much they can teach us.

They share a number of characteristics with the Harvard and New South Wales responders who have aged successfully. They are not only the privileged of our society, having had their share of struggle. They are not sickly people, although most do have some physical issues, which they manage without hindering a purposeful life. Over the years they have reinvented themselves a number of times; they have continued to grow, restructuring their lives as circumstances change, and they show resilience in dealing with hardship. They have been adventurers and risk takers. A certain amount of good luck is involved in growing old without accident, disease or social catastrophe but some aspects of successful ageing are, in fact, negotiable. Perseverance and self-motivation are traits that are significantly associated with longevity. Successful long livers enjoy the company of others of all ages. They are community-minded and remain interested in politics and current affairs. They manage their routines and their needs independently and, although lonely from time to time, they take action and are not isolated. They are not consumed by regrets and have learned to live day by day, remaining interested and interesting. Throughout their lives they have felt loved and worthwhile. These are inspirational people, role models for life in the prime of old age. I want you to meet some of these individuals now.

PART TWO

THE
ELDERS

CHAPTER 5

THE POSTER GIRL

LESLEY FALLOON 1920 –

L ESLEY Falloon is a case study of how to live into your nineties. She has the attributes researchers cite as predictors of living to a ripe old age and is the kind of human being we admire at any age. She has had good health but her personality, imagination and determination have, despite personal loss and grief, created a life she describes as joyous. When Lesley turned 90 she had so many friends who wanted to celebrate with her she was thrown 16 parties. Lesley was educated as a scientist, unusual in her era, but she chose to work in voluntary organisations, as befitted her middle-class status, until her children had grown up. She reinvented her life repeatedly. She is looking for another career.

If ever there was a poster girl for old age Lesley

Yvonne Acrotriche Falloon is it. She added Acrotriche (the genus for 'little green flower') as a botany student at university when a friend decided to change her name from Jean to Jacaranda. Lesley went one better, choosing an exotic name nobody would have heard of. It's a decision that reflects this woman's sense of humour and her individualism.

Lesley is a fit, vigorous, inventive, fun-loving 93-year-old. Fate has been kind to her. She has had opportunities few women of her generation were given, has seldom suffered financial hardship and has been loved by parents, a husband, children and friends. These all made life easier, but Lesley's philosophy of life is her own creation; her determination, adaptability, and strength of character are the tools she has drawn on to reinvent herself. Social changes over 90 years have not left Lesley behind. She has repeatedly risen to meet challenges and been rewarded through her achievements. Her attitude to life is a model for any age.

Lesley is a positive person. If something is wrong she will act to alleviate the problem. She appreciates differences in others and has an open mind. She is ready to try new tasks—to give it a go. She says these qualities have strengthened with every passing year and as a result she says she has gained much.

I have known Lesley for more than 50 years. She has always been entertaining company: she has a face that lights up when she greets you, a vivacious friendly demeanour and a ready laugh. She makes it clear that she is happy to see you.

Lesley belongs to that generation of women who, once married, could not pursue a career because it was not thought proper to do so. Despite the fact she was well educated and highly qualified, as few women were then, there were many pressures exerted to prevent middle-class married women such as Lesley working. They did not have to work for economic reasons, and for what other reason would a woman want to work? Although women were expected to work during World War Two, social norms dictated that jobs be kept for the returning soldiers and that the women revert to domestic duties. Men were socialised to see themselves as the proper and sole providers for the family; if his wife worked, a man saw himself as a lesser person, diminished and shamed in his own eyes and in the eyes of his peers. Professional men's parents were horrified if their daughters-in-law worked. So with a husband she loved and in-laws opposed to her working in a paid job, Lesley found it easier to look for satisfaction in other ways and, as an agreeable and adaptable person, this was not difficult for her to do.

Things were different for single women, or 'old maids' as they were called. They could bear the stigma of work because they were considered unable to find a man to support them. I was on the cusp of this generation with two older sisters, one an office worker and one a hairdresser, who ceased working when they married and were homebodies thereafter. I chose to follow a different path.

There was no stigma attached to married women who took on voluntary work, and that was where Lesley began her career outside the family, finding an outlet for her talents. Eventually, as mores changed, Lesley adapted, seizing the opportunities that came her way. She was a natural leader and one experience would lead to another. Lesley had no difficulty finding ways to use her talents within the social strictures of her era while pushing boundaries as feminism splintered the glass ceiling and opened long closed doors.

She was born as Lesley Keipert in Ardrossan, South Australia, where her father had a medical practice. Later, her family went to live in the small town of Rupanyup, Victoria where she attended primary school. She had the advantage of growing up within a professional family. Her father wanted to make sure she had the best opportunities in life. Lesley was always encouraged to do what she wanted: 'What I did was up to me.' She was urged to take responsibility for her own actions and behaviour from the outset, a valuable lesson for every child to learn, but rather unusual in those days.

Lesley learned to be self-motivated. She liked to be top of her class and in Rupanyup she always was. She enjoyed working to win that position. She was an all-rounder who trained hard to be the top athlete in her school as well. She won the spelling competition at

Rupanyup and then won against Murtoa and Minyip, but lost in the bigger district competition. At 12 she was spelling words like 'pusillanimous' and 'heinous', words she claims she can't spell at 93. She found great joy in doing well: 'It was so much worth the effort'.

Her father Leslie was a country doctor—a surgeon, an obstetrician—one of a rare breed of doctors who 'did the lot'. He was an even-tempered man and Lesley loved him dearly. Her mother, Charlotte, was a nurse, an attractive woman, a great cook and for many years the champion doubles tennis player of the Wimmera. Lesley's beloved younger brother, christened James Ashton but called Dig, is now 90 and they remain in close contact. Her parents loved music and valued books. She grew up hearing the works of grand opera: there was a pianola in the house and singalongs are a fond memory.

Rupanyup was 'a good town to grow up in, with nice interesting people', and serviced a big grazing and farming district. The climate was ideal for outdoor sports; tennis, golf and quail-shooting were popular. Lesley recalls sitting on the side veranda of her home, reading or playing table tennis, the bees humming in the flowers. The family went on trips to Melbourne and had the use of a holiday house in the Grampians where she and her friends would climb peaks and swim in the creek pool. There was also an annual beach holiday to Erskine House, a fashionable resort at Lorne on the Victorian coast. 'It was a happy, enjoyable, active childhood', and also a privileged one.

She was a religious child, probably because her best friend was the daughter of the Methodist minister. While Lesley was allowed to do anything on a Sunday, her best friend was not. From this Lesley surmised she might not go to heaven. Although reassured by her father, she wasn't sure; perhaps her friend's father knew more about heaven than her own. The answer to her quandary, 80 years on, still lies somewhere in the future.

Lesley's second decade began at Murtoa Higher Elementary School, then she sat for scholarships to Presbyterian Ladies' College (PLC) and Methodist Ladies' College (MLC). She won a half scholarship to each school and, making her own choice, finally settled on PLC, becoming a boarder in Melbourne.

Lesley was interested in microbiology and biochemistry which became her majors in a Bachelor of Science degree at Melbourne University. She was awarded a Commonwealth Government Scholarship and applied to attend University Women's College (UWC), where she won an exhibition. It was a radical institution as the first college for women at Melbourne University and, in 1938, she was among the second intake of students, who were considered the best and brightest. There were only 33 young women, who formed a tight-knit group and remained friends throughout their lives. The atmosphere in college encouraged these privileged few to develop their independence and belief in themselves and their abilities—an area where Lesley had a headstart.

She remembers her upbringing and education as joyful and inspirational years:

> the family joys of success, the joys of university, of college, new friends, lovely boys and romances, new experiences—the ballet, theatre, restaurants, balls, parties—learning and more learning, achievement. The first college principal, Miss Williams, encouraged the girls to think of the inspiring spires of Oxford and Cambridge—of university life as a search for knowledge.

When I attended UWC, it was a similarly seminal experience.

In 1941, when Lesley graduated, it was expected that women would contribute to the war effort in the workforce. There was nothing unusual about a woman working when men were at war. She spent six months as a dietetic student at the Alfred Hospital and then worked for William Anglis and Company as a biochemist and microbiologist.

Her father died unexpectedly in 1942, when Lesley was 22. This was 'the most shattering experience'. She was 'overwhelmingly sad'. She had been close to her father and at 46 he was still a young man. This was the first blow in a joyful life.

In 1943, with a group of friends, Lesley helped to form the Past Students' Association of UWC to influence the future of the college and its choice of principal. Those who had attended UWC viewed college with great gratitude and nostalgia, recognising the major contribution it had made to their lives. They wanted to give something back. College became an absorbing social interest and a focus for acquiring business skills. She was elected the Past Student Representative on the Council in 1950 and later the Governors' Representative. She also held the offices of president and acting honorary treasurer. Between 1952 and 1980 she helped raise funds for the expansion of the college buildings, for furnishings and scholarships as well as for organising garden parties and picnic reunions.

In 1944 she began working for the Institute of Anatomy in Canberra, travelling around the country surveying the diet of the Australian population. She had a wonderful job but she had also fallen in love with a very exciting man, Edward E. M. Falloon (Ted), whom she had first met when he was studying at Ormond College, but who was now a soldier posted to New Britain. When he came home on leave Ted was Lesley's priority and she would scramble her plans to make sure she could see him. Working in country South Australia, with wartime restrictions on interstate travel, meant 'monumental string-pulling to get home to Melbourne to meet him'. They married and her job became untenable so she worked as a microbiologist and biochemist for H. Mortensen, a urologist in Collins Street. She resigned when her husband returned home in 1946.

The end of the war and the reuniting of family and friends that followed was an exciting time.

> When one's husband is a soldier, and in danger, it alters one's thinking. I felt my first responsibility was to him, to make him happy after all the horrors of war. Everyone was in the same boat, finding somewhere to live, being joyous about finding a place with a refrigerator—what bliss! Furnishing with the family hand-me-downs; holding parties to celebrate returning to Melbourne for all our friends in the forces; then pregnancies.

This was the generation that gave birth to the Baby Boomers. 'It was marvellous to have a partner to share life and plan a future, to test ideas, to laugh together, to tell you how you looked.'

They lived in the Dandenongs for a month until deciding on a house in Burwood. Ted became very ill with malaria in 1947, but recovered and bought a dental practice in Sandringham.

Their first child was a girl, Janet, born in 1947. The birth was an exciting event as Janet was the first grandchild on both sides of the family. A son, James, was born in 1949 and he also brought great happiness. Family has been a central focus of Lesley's full and busy life.

I don't think, in spite of the interminable gestation period of nine months, that I was in any way prepared for the miracle of our firstborn. It is quite unbelievable when one first sees that exceptional tiny child, very much alive, with perfect toes and fingernails, fat cheeks and large navy blue eyes, looking at you appraisingly, thinking, 'Are you good enough for me to spend the rest of my life with you?' I sincerely hope she [Janet] thinks she made the right decision. This wonderful feeling of privilege and the viewing of a miracle occurred again with the birth of our next child.

In the ensuing years there may sometimes be an occasional doubt about miracles but then the superb grandchildren arrive and life reinvents itself. In my older years I feel even more strongly the paramount importance of my family and I see it again and again with my friends. I feel great sympathy for those who are unlucky enough not to have a family. As well as all the love and affection and consideration they engender, because of them we retain great interest and involvement in the future, their future.

As a good wife, Lesley built her world around her children and found satisfying interests (including the work for UWC) that complemented family life. She maintained her academic interests by joining the Lyceum Club, for female graduates, and balanced that interest by playing sport.

In 1956 the family moved to Hampton into a large house with a large garden. They had chooks, bantams, a dog, cat, rabbit, ducks, budgerigars and a bathing box on the beach. It was an 'idyllic life'. Ted believed in doing what they wanted to do 'now'. Lesley thought they might finish in the bankruptcy court but 'we did things at the right time'. With this move to a new area Lesley became very involved with local affairs, becoming the treasurer of the fund-raising committee to build Sandringham Hospital, a large undertaking.

As always, she enjoyed a wide-ranging social life and entertained with dinner and luncheon parties. With Ted she joined the National Gallery Society and the Melbourne Theatre Company. They were foundation members of the Melbourne Film Society and regularly attended the ballet. She was invited to join Riversdale Golf Club in 1956 and the Royal Melbourne Golf Club in 1961. She became a council member of the Royal Melbourne Golf Club Associates from 1971 to 1972.

In those same years Lesley became involved in a historic fight to save a wonderful row of mahogany gum trees in Linacre Road, Hampton. Council wanted to widen the road and claimed the trees were diseased. Lesley phoned a friend who was a professor of botany and asked him to send down the best plant pathologist in Melbourne to look at the trees. The pathologist reported that the trees were healthy, but his report was ignored by the Sandringham Council. 'So it was war.'

Public meetings were held, guards were placed on the trees for 24 hours a day, and they employed a top-line barrister to match the council's barrister. They raised money, held dinners, had artists paint the trees and sold the pictures at art shows. After nine appearances in the Supreme Court they won the case in a very public battle which became a cause célèbre, and a prime example that the 'little man could win' and 'how important it was for councils to listen to constituents and have an open mind'. Two councillors lost their seats in subsequent elections. Out of this activity the Hampton Conservation and Planning Association was born. Lesley was its vice-president for three years. She was asked to stand for Council but refused.

With the skills Lesley obtained through volunteering in a range of areas, she likened herself to a managing director running a variety of activities in diverse organisations. She had excellent instincts and became a good strategic thinker. She was not afraid to take the lead and stand up for what she believed was right. She was a logical, forthright, lively speaker with charisma: a good mix for a CEO or an activist.

For more than two decades Lesley enjoyed this style of living—active in sport, involved in honorary community work and caring for her family. Her husband was successful in his profession and comfortable with Lesley's activities, and they were very happy together. But when her children were in their teens Lesley began to crave a new challenge and thought about returning to paid employment. She wanted to use the skills she had developed.

In 1965, a seminar was held at UWC called 'Leading a Double Life'. Its purpose was to discuss how women who had been trained as professionals could re-enter the workforce after a long absence. The keynote speaker was Dora Bialestock, a GP who practised with her husband. Dr Bialestock was a small dynamic woman who spoke of the way she managed her roles as wife, mother and busy medical practitioner. I attended the seminar as a mother of two very young children. I intended to work and was enthralled listening to Dora speak about the way she organised her life. I went up to Dora after her address and said, 'I'm going to do what you are doing.' She looked at me and said bluntly, 'But you are not, are you?' I was taken aback and thought to myself, 'But I will be, and soon.'

Lesley and her friends had a different view. They were rather horrified by the lifestyle the lively doctor painted. Lesley says:

> I don't think I was driven by women's liberation
> to join the workforce. I had always been liberated.
> We had been brought up in the knowledge that
> we were most fortunate people and must give,
> as we had been given, back to the community
> according to our talents. We had two missionaries
> on my father's side, and my mother's brother, after

graduating in medicine, paid for his two younger sisters' education.

So by the time Betty Friedan came along [with *The Feminine Mystique*] I was already doing my bit, apart from being a wife and mother. My generation at 'Leading a Double Life' was appalled at the apparently very mechanical organisation required by Dora to lead her life, and had no great desire to live like that.

I was determined always that I would use my abilities in what I had been trained to do. But when I found what was required for me to return to my profession I could see my learned skills over the years were with people—so I later did social work for that reason. And although we despised social workers (a bit) at the university it certainly was a good choice, if not financially, then in achievement and satisfaction. In hindsight I should have done an MBA—same result but more money—next time, perhaps.

Betty Friedan's *The Feminine Mystique* had been published in 1963 and led to volatile discussions about the roles of women. The book helped trigger a revolution among many who had remained as housewives, or who had not received higher education or an opportunity to work in a profession. They suffered what Friedan called 'the problem that has no name'. The discussion was broadened in 1970 with the publication of Germaine Greer's *The Female Eunuch*, and again in 1975 with Anne

Summers' book *Damned Whores and God's Police*.

Lesley had always felt liberated but realised: 'I was a most fortunate woman compared to many of my "sisters". Later as a councillor, while I represented all people, I was able to ensure women as far as possible got an equal go.'

In this changing social context, she received a call from a friend who was based in the Biochemistry School at Melbourne University working in the Growth Study Unit in the Anatomy School.

> She was pregnant and asked me to take her place for six to nine months when she had the baby. I said I could not possibly as I had been away from such work for a long time. She said she had discussed this with the professor and we would have a week together before she left me to it. I was quite overwhelmed by such confidence in me. After seeking more reassurance from her—the job would entail three days a week from 9.30am to 4.00pm so my children would not be alone after school—I accepted.
>
> When my husband came home I was bubbling with excitement. 'Guess what? I have a part-time job in the Anatomy and Biochemistry Schools.' He thought at first I was joking, then, was horrified. 'Why would you want a job? We don't need you to work. It is quite ridiculous. You won't take it of course.'
>
> I said, 'I have already accepted because I thought you would be happy for me to do what I have been trained to do.'

'Well, I think it's quite ridiculous and disastrous from a taxation point of view.' Of course, I stuck to my word. I learned so much and enjoyed the work. I did not take long to learn and know what I was doing. But I refused when offered the job permanently. I knew I needed something more challenging and with more variety. Also the home front was *not* supportive—the gains were not sufficient. It was rewarding to know I could do it—I had proved to myself I could do it.

While Lesley decided the family would come first in this instance, this job was to be her transition to work and further study. She had great autonomy and authority as a housewife and had wonderful opportunities to engage and achieve, but the time had come for an independent woman like her, whose children were off her hands, to take on the challenge of the workforce. Staying at home was not something Lesley had ever felt the need to apologise for but she was eager to use her training and skills elsewhere.

In 1973, at the age of 53 and with her children in their late twenties, Lesley decided to return to study, undertaking a one-year social welfare course and move into a higher gear.

My desire to return to the workforce was purely to use the skills I had been trained to use—it seemed improper to do otherwise. I would undertake further study and would move into an arts faculty.

It seemed very attractive: rather than returning
to peering down a microscope I would work with
people. Also science had moved on so fast that I
would need retraining. I certainly made the right
choice: social work, community organisation,
helping people to initiate and cope with change
were all complementary.

For six years up to the 1980s Lesley was a part-time
social worker at the Mount Royal Day Hospital, where
she arranged educational lecture series for relatives of
day-hospital patients. She became active in public health,
ageing and disability issues related to social work. She
helped establish a committee which successfully lobbied
government to introduce for older citizens reduced
public transport fares, half-price taxis and wheelchair
taxis.

Ironically, Lesley's dear husband was proud of her
career. Social mores had changed and for a man in his
fifties to have a professional working wife in the late
1970s and 1980s was considered very progressive. Ted had
warmed to the idea: with support at home there was no
stopping Lesley.

In 1978, at the age of 58, she launched into another
stage of her life as an elected councillor for the City of
Sandringham. Lesley says she was tricked into standing
for council at a by-election. The experience of fighting
for the Linacre Road trees, for which she attended 'so
many boring council meetings', turned her off the idea

of running for office. She refused all invitations to stand but is now grateful she did. She loved having the ability to change things for the better and served for five terms from 1978 to 1992, as mayor from 1982 to 1983. As Mayor she chaired all major council committees and many community committees while continuing to work part-time as a social worker.

In 1980 she also chaired the South Eastern Weights and Measures Union for a year and was a member for three years. The Union served thirteen councils and employed two inspectors who would travel around, checking the accuracy of butcher and grocer scales and petrol bowsers. 'It was like an old-world London Board of Management. We met in a splendid room, each with our notepads and individual cigarette supply. New councillors were given the role as it was considered monumentally boring, but I found it fascinating.'

Lesley was still on the council when Ted died from cancer of the jaw in 1989. He had worked in his practice until a week before his death. His loss was 'unbearable at times' but her life was busy and interesting. She was 68. She reflected on her future and said to herself: 'You've got to pull your finger out and get back to work or resign.'

Lesley's CV gives some idea of the breadth of involvement she brought to the local council. Council work was voluntary apart from a small emolument, paid in her later years, to cover phone and stamps. Lesley did not mind being unpaid; she had all the status and money she needed to do the best job she could. And, as she says, 'payment in more recent years has not made for better councils'.

In 1985 Lesley added a new dimension to her life by becoming a marriage celebrant. She named children as well as conducting marriages but did not perform funerals. There were so many highlights in those years.

> I went everywhere for marriage venues— marvellous hotels and reception centres, humble backyards where I had to gently remonstrate against paling fences as a wedding background, wonderful gardens, boats. I think I was very successful in encouraging my participants to think of the commitment, the permanence, the giving, and to make their marriage ceremony something of great importance.
>
> It was a very satisfying role and provided me with some wonderful memories. An elderly couple at our first meeting asked if the marriage could be held in my house, could I provide the witnesses; there would be no family or friends at the wedding. I said I would be very happy to have some dozen or so of their family and friends as guests in my house. 'Oh no,' they said, 'the wedding must be secret; you see, we are marrying because we don't want our grandchildren to know we have been living in sin all these years.'

Lesley resigned from this career at 89 years of age in 2009, after 24 years and hundreds of ceremonies.

So how does one assess such an active life and the influence of its contribution on longevity? It is not surprising that someone with such a positive approach to life and a remarkable ability to reinvent herself lives long. While health is a huge factor, and Lesley has had no illnesses to hold her back, a positive attitude to life has been a driving force. Lesley attributes her long life to:

wonderful parents, great genes. I am so very healthy, strong bones, never sick; loving family, supportive when needed, otherwise I think they see me as indestructible; wonderful friends, and lots of admiration which is wonderful, so heart-warming; it gives satisfaction. I try to give my best shot at what I do. Since my 90th birthday everyone knows I'm over 90. Before, they thought I was years younger and now I am covered with plaudits and affection.

What is important to her as the end of life approaches?

Probably coming to terms with oneself, with all my imperfections, the mistakes I have made where I could have been so much better, kinder in my dealings with my family and others. Forget all that, I enjoy what is left. I have so many interests. I can't help being busy. I always have something I want to do. I'm a dinosaur with the computer, I'm left behind but it doesn't worry me. I'm good enough in other fields of endeavour to hold my own. There is always some unfinished interest—a great book, an article to write, a letter, a phone call to divert me, a holiday, a friend in need, the theatre. There just isn't enough time in the day, the week, the year.

I meet once a month with women in search of excellence (WISE); we have a speaker. I meet a group for coffee each Saturday and work in the op shop once a month.

What has Lesley valued most?

I've been lucky all my life. I attract happy people. I have valued my parents, brother, childhood, good attitudes, education, university, dear husband and children, intact extended family, incredible opportunities, my philosophy—all positive.

I value integrity, loyalty, those whose word is their bond. The company and discussions with, and ideas of, intelligent people, the ability to change things, the love and friendship of family and friends, the ability to read, argue, listen and learn— democracy and politics...I appreciate the gift of life so much—the beauty of sunny days, of nature, of animals, of the sea and the stars. What is going to happen if we don't take care of it?

Lesley packs every week of her life with activities and social contact. She takes care of people, she cooks, she drives, she organises, she shops, she helps out in all kinds of ways. She visits those less fortunate; people enjoy her company and seek her out. She is rarely alone and never lonely. She always has a smile, a laugh, and an interest in

everything and everybody. It has been her way of life for
92 years and ageing has not changed this.

The circumstances that have caused Lesley most
pain are the loss of family:

> The death of my father in 1942, the death of my
> son James from a heart attack at age 55 in 2004. My
> husband and my mother's deaths were releases
> and therefore a little mitigated. The death of my
> son-in-law aged 42 was so sad for my daughter and
> grandchildren.
>
> My aged peers are often very frail and depend
> on me a lot for company, phone calls, etc. Some
> are wonderful with great minds and great ideas.
> We share so much. Sometimes I get worn out with
> visiting hospitals and ringing people up. Some ask a
> lot of me. I realise it is essential to have friends right
> across the age spectrum. Ultimately we have to be
> responsible for ourselves.
>
> My closest friends vary from 50 to 94. I have a
> group of women sixtyish, wonderful company,
> nearly all retired. At the age of 93 obviously most of
> my life is behind me but I don't even think of that, it
> is what is ahead and inside me which is important.
> I have just recently suffered from arthritis of the
> knees. It is a shock. I have walked so freely all my
> life but, strangely, I just accept it as part of life.
>
> I very much hope I will die before I become
> decrepit. If not I hope I will never whinge, or talk
> about my ailments. I will have a dog and cat for
> company and champagne together when you visit.

If you don't I will have a glass by myself and wear pretty clothes. I hope my sight will always allow me to read. I want to live in my own home. We all have to think about death at times, our will and our funeral, our affairs and possessions. The older one gets—I think age induces complete acceptance of death. I believe we should all have the right to end our own life when we feel the time is right but great care is needed to protect the vulnerable against predatory people.

There is appalling ageism in the media amongst young people about their own ageing. I try to be a strong disciple about the advantages of ageing.

Lesley's doctor told her recently she will live to be 100 and Lesley nearly fell off her chair. 'I have a lovely life but I am not playing bridge and going to my dear friends' funerals for the next ten years; I need a new career!'

Lesley will undoubtedly reinvent herself.

CHAPTER 6

THE OLDEST SKYDIVER IN THE WORLD

JAMES BRIERLEY 1924−

A T 89, Jim Brierley is the youngster in this book. He achieved fame late in life *because* he was old and still jumping from planes. His feats and escapades have become legendary. He is a classic example of someone who has reinvented himself many times in his work and his private life following trauma and cultural change. Throughout his careers he has been described as an exceptionally forceful character, highly intelligent, ever resourceful, absolutely trustworthy and reliable: not a man to be ignored, an asset to his friends and associates. He was always there pushing the plane into the hangar at the end of the day while others were busy drinking. If he could do it all again what would he do differently? 'Not a damned thing, actually.'

Every weekend for nearly three decades, weather permitting, Jim Brierley has driven from Phillip Island to Tooradin in Victoria to join a group of about 30 skydivers. They share a culture that has become an important part of Jim's life. At 89 he is the oldest active skydiver in the world. Stories abound about the daft things he has done. Others want to jump with him to share the fame. They all have a kind word to say about him, the blokes as well as the women, who hug him like a cuddly bear. He is an outrageous flirt but does it with such class that the club women love him. Jim decided he would celebrate his 88th birthday with his final jump, and members of the club drew lots to jump with him. The winners leapt out together in formation and then the members held a barbecue to acknowledge his achievement. He is the club's popular daredevil hero, who continues to sneak in an extra jump since his so-called finale.

A paratrooper in World War Two, Jim has completed more than 3200 jumps since he took up jumping again in 1983, aged 58, after his first wife, Jean, died of breast cancer. Some sceptics considered him too old to take up such a dangerous pastime.

Jim is regarded as a true gentleman of the sport, whose achievements have been recognised in a series of landmark jumps by his fellow jumpers. To celebrate his 80th birthday he was joined by 80 skydivers in

Toogoolawah's Equinox Boogie in Queensland. His 3000th jump was a media event, covered by radio, television and the press. It was a dark, cloudy day but the grey skies did not deter the veteran. When he landed after the big jump he quipped, with typical understatement, 'It gets me out of the domestic chores at home, and I like skydiving better than gardening.'

The higher up the plane flies before a skydiver jumps, the longer the freefall, which is the time to play around before you dock into an agreed formation. Jim recalls a night jump at Pakenham where:

> we jumped out at 12,000 feet. It takes 30 minutes in the plane to reach that height and there is a 60-second freefall at 12,000. We planned an eight-way formation and by 9000 feet we were all in it. It was a phenomenal jump. There we were. All eight of us joined in a star formation, just grinning like idiots thinking how good we were.

Jim has jumped all over the globe. One memorable moment was jumping out of a massive Hercules plane in Bali. 'There were over 500 skydivers from America and around the world. We were jumping from 13,000 feet. Due to the prevailing winds offshore we went out over the ocean to come in with the sea breeze and when the huge door opened it was such an amazing sight!' He was one of 10 Australians who jumped into Wadi Rum, a valley in the mountains of Jordan where *Lawrence of Arabia* was filmed; he was a member of a four-way jump that created a world record by over 70-year-olds in Canada. He competed in the Master Games in 2001 and jumped into the MCG before a Grand Final in 1995. His highest jump was from 25,500 feet when he was aged 76. The freefall at that height was two minutes, three seconds.

Jim has taken risks in his time, jumping off Melbourne's Westgate Bridge on his 70th birthday, and some of the thrills have resulted in spills, some serious: all have added to his legendary status. If a main chute line gets tangled when opening you have to cut it away to release your reserve chute. This has happened to Jim a number of times. He used to shut down his canopy and ride the flapping chute down before letting the toggles up at 600 feet 'just for the hell of it'.

He's infamous for one cutaway reported by the Drop Zone Safety Officer as so low his view was obscured by a bush. One time he cut away and went for the reserve but nothing happened. He thought, 'Well, this is it, Jim', but then he felt a gentle tug and the chute finally opened. Another time he rigged his chute back-to-front to see how he would manage the fall. He had seen an American fly his canopy backwards and thought he would like to give it a try, but it did not go according to expectations and he landed in the Barastoc seed factory in Pakenham after just managing to open his reserve chute at a very low altitude. He has on another occasion landed in the middle of a freeway, and once in mangroves.

Jim has broken his wrist, his leg and his back, with three wedge fractures and loss of fins on his vertebrae. On that occasion, Jim was doing a six-way jump and had been warned that the winds were very strong. The others were unhurt but Jim landed so heavily he made a deep impression with his footprints in the ground—so deep one of the others thought it worth photographing. In 1983 Jim fell back on landing, cracking his skull and causing a blood clot (a sub-dural haematoma) and loss of speech for a time. He drove himself to the hospital, having a minor accident on the way.

After some 28 incident reports Jim was called before the Discipline Committee and given a life suspension. He appealed and was allowed to jump pending the outcome. The verdict that allowed him to continue was hedged with seven strict conditions which were dropped after two years.

But no misadventure has deterred Jim from continuing to jump. With a fractured back he jumped in a support brace. There is nothing else in his life that compares to the exhilaration he feels skydiving or to the friendship of the young men and women who share the jumping experience. They revere Jim, want to jump with him and share his triumphs. They are his extended family. But these days he doesn't play up and take risks.

His second wife, Barbara, shares a happy relationship with Jim and supports his skydiving exploits. She is philosophical about his adventures, saying that if she gets a call from Jim from the hospital she knows at least that he is alive. Barbara is not averse to taking a few risks herself, joining Jim in the longest bungee jump in the Southern Hemisphere, in New Zealand in 2002, at the age of 66. Jim jumps fewer times each weekend than he used to and pays to get his chute packed now. He is stiffer and a little slower to move in the plane. He grunts and groans when the landings aren't as graceful as he'd like.

Jim has been a POP, a parachutist over phorty, an SOS, skydiver over 60, and a JOS, jumper over 70. He's now a JOE and aims to be a JON, a jumper over 90, as he continues to accumulate more jumps, and receive fewer incident reports and injuries in a remarkable skydiving career. He once thought that when he gave up skydiving golf would fill the vacuum, but he gave up golf and the skydiving continued. When asked by a journalist, 'With your years of experience both in the sport and of life generally, what advice would you give to the people who currently run skydiving in Australia?' Jim replied, 'Renew my licence.'

Jim was born in 1924 in British India, now Pakistan, where his father was serving in the army. He lived there for 10 years and was admitted to the military boarding school, Mt Abu Lawrence, in Rajputana at the age of five. He was moved to Aden, in South Arabia, in 1936. Later that year he and his older brother, who kept a look out for Jim, were sent to the Duke of York's

Royal Military School in Dover in the UK.

Although he had four brothers and a sister, he remembers little of family life before his school years; once at school he rarely saw his mother. Parents would attend on Founder's Day and he would go home once a year for holidays. His father would be 'all over us for about three days then he would have had a "bellyful" and tell us to get outside and enjoy God's fresh air'. Jim saw himself as a quiet, unadventurous kid, a conformist— not an army brat—who learned self-reliance. He was inward-looking, a loner.

For six years between 1938 and 1944 Jim did not see his mother at all. When she did see him again she hardly recognised the tall, handsome man he had become. During his school years he received an eclectic education and learned a trade. He became a boy soldier at 14 in the British Army Engineers, initially based at Kitchener Barracks and Fort Darland Technical School and, later, at Chepstowe Technical College, followed by sappers' training in Clitheroe, Lancashire, and the School of Military Engineering in Chatham. In these institutions the older boys brutalised the younger ones. Jim joined the boxing squad to learn to look after himself and became a Super Flyweight; he had no trouble with bullying after that.

When World War Two broke out Jim volunteered. He trained as an army engineer learning to build and blow up bridges. In 1942, when he was 18, he was shipped off to the Middle East, dodging U-boats on the way.

A call went out for volunteers for the F Squadron (later called 4th Squadron) in Kabrit, Egypt, which was for parachute engineers. Jim didn't know exactly what was involved but he was eager for adventure and ready to take on something new. The work included the use of explosives, lifting and laying mines, building assault bridges and roads of all kinds—as well as jumping out of planes. It was an exciting life for a young man.

In his three years with the parachute engineers and an engineering field company Jim made 18 training and two operational jumps serving in the Middle East, North Africa and the Central Mediterranean. At one point, nearing the end of the Italian campaign, his unit was 20 minutes away from taking off for a planned drop onto Field Marshal Kesselring's Italian headquarters, but it was aborted when the Germans got wind of the operation. The brigadier had joked that any survivors from the mission would fit in a jeep.

A few of the early operational jumps, according to Jim, were 'balls-ups' because young American pilots, still learning the ropes, would scatter the troops higher than the planned 800–1100-feet exit. For his service during World War Two Jim was highly decorated.

Jim had always stood up for himself and he rebelled when not accorded fair status. After the war, he first learned the art of using the media to his advantage. He was in Kenya and wanted out of the army. But the army refused to release him so Jim induced a British newspaper to take up his cause. In 1948 he became the first postwar regular soldier in East Africa to purchase his release at a price of £100. He was a strong, healthy 24-year-old by then, with no paper qualifications but considerable experience. His Certificate of Service in the British Army testified that Jim 'has an exceptionally forceful character, is very highly intelligent and is absolutely trustworthy and reliable'. That sums up Jim's character throughout his life.

Ever resourceful, he followed the army with a construction career in Kenya and Uganda. In 1949 he met Jean Hutchens, an English girl working in Kampala. They married in 1950 and lived in Uganda in a male-dominated, typically colonial society for 14 years. They had a core of friends who visited one another's houses. Europeans were in short supply; most of the labourers were African and the tradesmen were Indians.

Jim had a more responsible attitude to life as a married man but he describes his years with Jean as Jim Mark 1.

There was a Blue Book in the Colonial Service, issued every six months, which listed government servants in order of seniority, complete with titles, positions and qualifications. This was often used as a reference to decide whom to invite to functions. Jim wasn't always invited to certain events. The wives were the snobbiest, particularly on up-country stations. Jean was a feisty young woman who worked and was not too bothered by such behaviour, but Jim resented it. He decided to study the Swahili, Luganda and Rutoro languages so that this information in the Blue Book would give him added cachet.

He was not a man to be ignored; he was decisive and got the necessary job done. A striking example of Jim's problem-solving approach is drawn from his time in Uganda.

> We were stationed at a place called Masaka when I was Inspector of Works (Building) and Jean was working as secretary to the Assistant Resident (Senior Administrator for the district).
>
> Police special branch had alerted the government to the likelihood of a serious outbreak of civil disturbance and, as a result, a state of emergency was declared. Overnight I found myself summarily promoted to the positions of Inspector of Works (Plumbing, Electrical and Roads) as well as Building, plus Inspector of Explosives and Town Engineer.
>
> One of the major problems for central government in maintaining control was the rapid deployment of troops to the area but, because of the lack of an airstrip and the fact that Masaka was surrounded by swampy country, this meant looking for alternative possibilities. One was levelling the top of a 'mesa'-type hill situated about a mile and a quarter from the township and turning it into an airstrip capable of taking light planes.

In my new role of being responsible for everything concerning public works, I decided to halt a major roads contract and ordered the contractor to bring in his earth-moving equipment as well as all the explosives. They immediately began levelling the top of the hill and, within three days, we had an operational airstrip about 750 yards long. Jean recalled that the Assistant Resident, watching the cloud of dust over the hill, said that 'Jim would either get the OBE or the sack!' I telexed the Minister that an airstrip was now available for use and that the police should send a plane down to check it out. This was followed by the King's African Rifles (KAR) deploying a number of troops using Pioneer aircraft (with short take-off and landing capability). The insurrection subsided and I received a dressing-down from the Director for getting in touch with the Minister, who was an African in the first interim self-government before independence. I also received a bill from the government for the cost of using the contractor's equipment. I never paid it.

Shortly afterwards I successfully applied for a position with the Uganda Broadcasting Service and, with the promotion, gained an increase in salary as well as relocation back to Kampala.

I don't think I was missed by the Public Works Department but the new Assistant Resident for the Masaka District wrote to me personally to say that I would always be remembered for building the new Magistrate Courts and for the local airstrip.

Jim worked for two years as an on-air announcer and interviewer, collecting, researching and producing indigenous program material. He wanted a family but Jean resisted and they had only one daughter, named Zeb—the apple of Jim's eye. When the political situation in Uganda changed as independence and self-government became a reality, Europeans were put on notice. Only Africans would be promoted. Their daughter's future influenced their decision to move to Australia instead of South Africa, Canada or the United States. Although it was considered a tough place to be, Australia was regarded as safe.

In 1963 Jim arrived in Melbourne with a letter of introduction to John Guest, of Guest Biscuits, from the Commissioner of Police. It was an introduction that served him well. After advising Jim to remove his union activities from his CV, Guest helped to secure him a job at the ABC as an announcer with Radio Australia and Regional Australia. Jim had the right cultivated English accent for the ABC of that era. He worked on regularly rotating shifts, occasionally read the early morning news and introduced commentaries. With a secure job he sent for Jean and Zeb, who had been living in the UK. So the family settled in Melbourne and bought a new home in Balwyn.

In 1964 Jim applied successfully for a job at Monash University as Assistant to the Buildings Officer. Not long after that he became Director of Property for the

Australian Wool Board. For the next 15 years he worked for the Australian Wool Board and Wool Corporation, becoming the National Property Manager in 1974.

Jean worked with me at La Trobe University, as Secretary to the Centre for the Study of Media and Communication, which I began. She was a strong, opinionated woman, with clear likes and dislikes, who was angry about discrimination and injustice. She was an extremely competent assistant, and would refuse to work for people she did not respect. We got along famously and became good friends. At the time I was compiling the book *Media She* about the way women were demeaned in media coverage. Jean collected items for the book with great enthusiasm. Through her I met Jim, and for some months we were part of a golfing foursome, playing with the school dean and another academic friend once a week. I found Jim reserved and very gentlemanly as a golfing partner.

Jean's feminist leanings led her to take on a higher degree as a mature-aged student. She was particularly interested in history and Jim encouraged her to leave work for full-time study. I lost an excellent secretary but we remained good friends. Jean had gone through breast cancer before she worked with me and unfortunately it was another cancer in the other breast that led to her death. She died in 1982 after 32 years of marriage, and Jim cared for her throughout her final illness. It was the first time I had lost a friend through death: Jim asked me to speak at the funeral, and I did, with emotion and difficulty.

It was after Jean's death, in 1983, that Jim decided to take up skydiving—his last jump had been in 1944. He says he felt released from the strict code of behaviour he had conformed to with Jean and he 'could spread his wings and do what he wanted'. It was during this time that Jim ended up in hospital after a delayed parachute opening led to a heavy fall and a blood clot on his brain. When I saw him in hospital I feared the worst but I underestimated his strength and determination.

When he recovered I decided to introduce Jim to my good friend Barbara O'Connor, whom I had met in hospital when we each had our first child a few days apart. We had been friends for decades and I had shared Barbara's turmoil when she left her husband. She was a highly intelligent woman who wanted more from life than domestic service. She enrolled at La Trobe University to pursue a higher degree and a teaching career, which she achieved. Her subsequent partnership had not worked out and she was ready to meet someone new. Dinner at our house brought her together with Jim and their friendship blossomed.

One evening Barb and I had dinner in the city and, over a few glasses of wine, decided Jim needed a nudge. Together we drove to Lower Templestowe, where Jim was living, and invaded his house to ask when he intended to pop the question. He took our proposal with good grace. The nudge was all that was needed. They married in January 1987 and it is a partnership that has worked well for both of them over 25 years.

Jim describes his years with Barbara as Jim Mark 2. He is much mellowed and content with life, not so critical, angry and suppressed. 'We all pick up lessons en route in life.' He sees the price of a long life as 'anonymity'. He believes a major part of living is seeking recognition and that we make an effort to prolong our visibility. And visibility is certainly what Jim once craved when he was not given his due. He is secure now in the knowledge that he is not only the oldest active skydiver in the world, but he is also respected by those who share his world.

Skydiving remains important to Jim. His interest has kept him young at heart if not in body. The younger skydivers at Tooradin look after him, positioning him in the plane near the door so he can get out more easily.

He goes to the gym two or three times a week to maintain strength. He uses the computer to keep in touch with friends and is a hub for the circulation of jokes. He enjoys staying acquainted with the world. At the weekend he and Barbara do the crosswords.

Jim stays occupied and is never bored. He potters around the garden, keeps a meticulously tidy workshop in his garage. He reads lots of books, which Barbara, who is an avid reader, selects for him. He attends some University of the Third Age courses, and when Barbara taught her course on the Renaissance a year ago he acted as an assistant.

When Barb and Jim married, and the question of skydiving was raised, Barb said facetiously that Jim could keep jumping but should not expect her to take care of him if he were seriously injured. Ironically, it is Jim who has been the carer: Barbara has had a number of serious operations on her back, for a degenerative spinal condition, which have left her with intense pain to be managed. She remains fiercely independent, works to maintain her health and succeeds in doing more than most who have no disability to stop them. She is the organiser in their lives, managing the house, their social activities and their travel. Jim is grateful for his wife's initiative.

Jim has done nothing special to prolong his life. 'It must be in the genes,' he says. 'I appreciate each day once I am awake. I look out and see another day, another life. There is always something to do...I'm reaching the stage where I am outliving my family. My brother's gone. I am rounding off my life and chugging along. I don't have the same energy or stamina but I have no major health problems except for the scars from injuries.'

Death does not worry him; his only concern is what he will leave behind. He wants to make sure his daughter Zeb is well placed and Barbara is ensconced in an apartment in the city, near her two children and grandchildren. They live in the small community of

Phillip Island, among a large retired group of friends. Friends are not as important to Jim as they are to Barb but Barb's kids are his friends. He sees it as a lack of loyalty on his part that he tends to lose touch with others who may have once been important to him. He is still like that self-contained child who was booted out of home at five years old, no longer a member of an intimate family.

Yet he still writes an email each week to an old army friend, Eddie, who was in the 3rd Parachute Squadron in the UK. Eddie was part of the D-Day drop in Normandy and jumped in the Rhine River crossing. They did not meet again for 47 years, until there was a reunion in Chatham for boy soldiers in 1989. Jim sat next to his 'best friend' and couldn't remember him.

Jim has regretted not being part of a supportive family. Jean did not want kids but 'it's too late for bitterness'. Both marriages and his daughter have given him the most meaning in his life. When I ask, 'In an ideal world how would you like to spend your final years?' He replies, 'With my wife.'

He and Barb are good friends still enjoying sharing adventures in old age. Marriage provides them with excellent companionship, as it does for most couples who have stayed together through long lives.

CHAPTER 7

THE ADVOCATE

MARY OWEN 1921–

MARY Owen is a petite, feisty advocate for women and equality. At 92, she still looks lively and people rally around her. She lost her mother at age 16 months and her first replacement mother at four, and grew up searching for emotional support from a third 'mother'. From an early age she asserted her independence and applied herself to doing well at all she tried. She made the wrong choice in marrying an older man who proved incompatible, but forged her own life as a successful typist, stenographer, private secretary, door-to-door saleswoman and demonstrator before finding her niche within the union movement advocating for women's working conditions. In a packed and committed life she thinks old people are those who allow others to make their decisions. At 75 she fulfilled a lifelong desire when she strapped on a pair of rollerskates for a birthday photo opportunity. She is recognised as one of the significant figures in Australian feminist history.

When Mary Owen retired from paid work in 1986 her friends organised a dinner to mark her retirement. Five hundred and forty women attended that dinner at the Hawthorn Town Hall and another 200 had to be turned away for lack of space. Those who missed out were so disappointed that it was proposed there should be a dinner the following year. And so there was, every year for 20 years. The purpose of the dinner was to honour someone who had made a significant contribution to the status of women; it was a celebration of women working with and for women. There was always an excellent speaker but it wasn't the speakers who drew the women. They came to catch up with old mates and colleagues they hadn't seen since the year before, and they also met new women. It was an experience they valued and one that represented all Mary stands for.

Mary has been an activist all her life; she is a lively human being who has lost none of the passion that has driven her commitment to the fight to combat discrimination against women.

Mary Roberta Evans was born on 8 February 1921 to Tyrrell George Granville Evans and Mary Joyce Pitt Withers. She was the granddaughter of the artist Walter Withers, a well-known impressionist painter from the

Heidelberg School. She denies inheriting any of his talent. She was a toddler when her mother gave birth to her twin sisters. Seventeen days later, still in hospital, her mother got out of bed to go to the phone to speak to her husband, collapsed and died from acute heart failure.

Tyrrell was only 29 when his wife died. He was a returned soldier from World War One whose left arm had been amputated above the elbow as the result of shrapnel wounds. As he was left-handed, the loss was a great handicap. He worked as a secretary of a small company and received a part pension for war injuries but his income was modest and it was impossible for him to care for three young children.

When a series of carers, unable to cope with three demanding babies, handed in their resignations, Tyrrell's sister Olive did what was expected of female relatives and resigned from her secretarial position to become a mother for the three young girls. Mary remembers nothing of the next two years but has two photographs which remind her of the house in which they lived. She doesn't know whether she blotted out the memory of that period because she didn't like it or she was simply too young to remember. But those early years are critical in the development of any child and so they left their mark.

The twins naturally enough became the centre of attention. Mary, who was old enough to miss her mother and was being upstaged by two new members of the household, must have felt genuine loss.

In August 1925, when Mary was four and a half, she was introduced to a new home in Glen Iris, where her two sisters were already installed with her father and his new wife. She now had a third mother and was denied access to her second, Aunt Olive.

Mary didn't think much about the business of having three mothers until she learned about the Aboriginal and British children who were taken from their parents at an early age. She suspects it must have had an effect on her emotional development, but she isn't sure what that was. Given the course Mary's life took, it is easy to speculate that she learned early on to assert herself in the household, run by a stepmother who used to complain about Mary's argumentative nature and her leading the twins into mischief. Mary recalls being locked in the lavatory as punishment, the only room in the house that could be locked.

As an adult she can understand the decisions her father had to take in his predicament. Tyrrell was a sensitive, kindly, but 'proper' man, a product of his times.

> He had high moral standards—according to British principles, as he saw them—and we were expected to behave like young ladies. When disaster really struck with the death of his wife and he was left with three babies and the need to be at work all day to support them, it is not surprising that he soon married again. His second wife produced two more

children—another girl and then the long-awaited son.

There was always a distinction between us and our half-siblings. My sisters and I thought our stepmother treated us unfairly, and so she did; but I understood much later in life that she didn't realise she was doing this. She just naturally thought her own children were so much prettier and more desirable than we were. One thing Dad would not tolerate was any suggestion that she was unfair. He was eternally grateful to her for taking him (and us) on—and so he should have been.

We were all expected to kiss Mummy and Daddy before we went to bed at night, and I remember, when Dad had been out playing billiards or at club meetings and came home after we were in bed, he would do the rounds of all the children and kiss us as we slept. As I grew older I would pretend to be asleep because I think I was embarrassed and didn't know how to respond to this show of affection. I had the same feeling when my Aunt Gladys would hug me and kiss me.

Looking back, I was never taught to be affectionate. The goodnight kiss with parents was very formal. I don't remember my stepmother ever taking me on her lap or cuddling me in any way. I had been the only grandchild on both sides of the family until...the birth of the twins, and Granny Withers and my aunties doted on me. Then we had Aunt Olive, Dad's sister, looking after us for two years and she doted on us too. But when Dad remarried Aunt Olive was told to stay away until invited to visit. I can understand the thinking behind this now—that it would make things too difficult for the new stepmother if we kept wanting to be with our aunt, but Aunt Olive, who had cared for us, was shattered and never forgave Dad—nor has Olive's daughter—and I don't blame them.

In reviewing Mary's life—unsurprisingly, given the emotional turmoil of her early years—one pattern that emerges is her drive to be noticed and to succeed in all she does. This determination has helped make her an excellent salesperson and an outspoken lobbyist and has prepared her for the role she would take on in midlife, which brought her the most satisfaction, as an advocate for women.

Mary's stepmother did not neglect her education: she taught her to read before she started school at age six. Mary jumped kindergarten and went straight to Grade 1 at Korowa Church of England Girls' Grammar School. At 11, Mary was sent to Lauriston Girls School. She thinks she was moved because her parents didn't care for her friends at Korowa, at least not the friend with whom she spent the most time.

Mary got off to a bad start at her new school: she was to begin in the second term but developed chickenpox during the holidays and had to wait for two weeks after school reopened until she was no longer contagious. Feeling out of her depth in a new context, she hated school all that year. The girls in her class had been learning French for two years when Mary started and she was left behind, but by the second year she had settled in and began to love Lauriston.

There was little opportunity to meet with boys, and any she knew she thought rather silly. She didn't change that view even when she left school and used to play tennis with some of them at a friend's house. Boys her age seemed juvenile. She wasn't interested in watching their football matches or even the annual public schools' boat race. She much preferred to play sport herself or to read. She loved books and devoured them, particularly the classics: Greek myths and legends, Louisa May Alcott, *The Scarlet Pimpernel*, Frances Parkinson Keyes, *The Three Musketeers*, although she says she remembers precious little of them now. She wanted to be a writer.

> I never felt I could invite anyone home because my stepmother treated us differently from the way my friends' mothers treated them (and me) when I went to their homes. I learned ballroom dancing at school with the boys from one of the boys' schools—Wesley College, I think. Most of the boys hated having to attend these classes and were hopeless at dancing; they had no idea how to keep in time with the music. I actually liked dancing and, in the cold weather, we girls used to spend lunch hour dancing in the gym hall with each other. We had a wonderful pianist—Ethel Parnham—and when I

needed a partner to attend the end-of-school ball I had to rope in a cousin to escort me. He took me to a couple of other dances too and Dad lent him his car to take me to something at the Palais at St Kilda, but he wasn't much of a dancer.

I knew next to nothing about sex at this time—except the bare medical facts—and had no interest in cuddling with boys.

Mary was a perfectionist about everything she did. She valued her father's approval and the way to get that, she thought, was to show that she could do things better than anyone else could. That drive to be the best has influenced her most of her life.

Mary was smart and her teachers thought she should go to university, but few girls did in those days. She was also conscious that her father was waiting for her to leave school so that he could afford to send her young brother to Scotch College. So despite her outstanding academic performance at school—she was only 15 when she matriculated in English, Economics, European History, Latin, Maths I and Maths IV—she was sent to Dacomb Business College to learn typing, shorthand and elementary bookkeeping. It would have taken two more years before she could enter university, and the fees would have been higher than school fees, so the subject was never raised.

In the mid-twentieth century most people took it

for granted that the ultimate goal for a woman was to marry. Any skills training was seen as a stop-gap, simply for getting by until marriage and providing something to fall back on, if through misfortune she had to support herself. Mary, with her interest in writing, decided she would like to be a journalist but her father was not impressed with this idea. He believed there were some very undesirable characters in that field. So Mary went to business school. 'I just accepted this but thought I was pretty smart because I won a half-year scholarship to study typing, stenography and bookkeeping.'

Inevitably Mary ended up as a stenographer in an office. 'I was offered a job with Hemingway & Robertson Pty. Ltd., business tutors by correspondence. Within two years I was elevated to be the Executive Administrator's stenographer and given a rise in salary, so I thought I'd done pretty well.'

At 91, Mary is still a very pretty woman and would always have been attractive but she didn't see herself that way. Her stepmother made it plain to her that her own daughter was the pretty one of the family. As the eldest of four girls, Mary did not have the opportunity to meet many boys. She continued to live at home while she went to business college and her only contact with men was through a religious group.

The mother of one of her friends at school was involved with the Plymouth Brethren and used to hold Christian meetings at her house. Mary was invited to attend and each Thursday night she would go to her friend's for dinner. In her search for meaning, this group seemed to offer something she did not have. She was impressed by the ideas of a young man, Wally Pike, who, with his wife, had been a missionary with the China Inland Mission. He motivated Mary to join the Brethren and become a born-again Christian. She joined when she was 16 and was baptised, fully clothed, at the Brethren's room in the hall near Gardiner Railway Station. Mary became a Crusader for the Brethren. 'I really tried very hard to be a good Christian.' When she joined the Crusaders Mary met and spent time in the company of men.

> There were two boys I remember who showed some interest in me. One was, I think, organised by my aunt and his mother, a friend of my aunt. He had a job as projectionist at the local picture theatre in Ivanhoe, near where my aunt lived. I got a free ticket to a film and afterwards he walked me home to my aunt's place, where he gave me a peck on the cheek at the gate before he delivered me to the front door: all very proper. He was a nice young chap but I can't remember that we had anything to talk about.
>
> The other one I remember was in Sydney. He lived opposite another aunt in Ryde and I think she would have liked me to marry him. He was a very handsome chap and I thought he was very nice; he sent me a huge box of chocolates from Darrell Lea, long before they opened in Melbourne. He

became an officer in the army when war broke out, but by this time Richard Owen had asked me to commit to him and, although I wouldn't promise, I felt I shouldn't be considering anyone else seriously. I was very straight-laced and proper! That was my Christian ethic and how I construed the way I thought my father expected me to behave. And men were such gentlemen in those days that they would not dream of pitching in on another fellow's territory when they thought there was an arrangement.

Mary was 18 when she met her husband-to-be, Richard Owen, at the Brethren meetings, and she agreed to marry him although he was 14 years her senior. After meetings Mary, Richard and Wally Pike would often walk miles along Hotham Street and Williams Road to High Street, where they caught the Glen Iris tram, talking all the while about what it meant to be a real Christian. She thinks Richard's maturity made him seem more interesting than the boys she had met before.

Dick was pretty persistent. He seemed a good, clean, decent-living chap and he played a good game of tennis. What more could I want? Another young chap, who was the Church of England vicar in Montague, was also a persuading influence. I never made a conscious decision that I should get married, it just seemed to overtake me—especially when war came and people were being sent overseas.

Richard joined the navy to escape the army call-up, becoming a sub-lieutenant in the intelligence division. Richard and Mary got engaged and they married on 12 September 1942 when Mary was 21. Mary moved around Australia with her husband, finding work in each city during the war years; there was no problem getting a job in those times.

> I worked with an accountancy firm for a few weeks in Adelaide before Dick was sent back to Melbourne. Then I got a job with the Department of Labour and National Service in Melbourne and managed to get a transfer to Sydney as a clerk in the Staff Records Section; then to Brisbane as Personnel Officer in charge of the records section of the Adelaide Street Branch of the Allied Works Council when Dick was appointed to General MacArthur's staff in Brisbane. When he was sent to New Guinea I stayed in Brisbane until the war ended and then he was sent back to Sydney, where I got a job as personal secretary to a consulting accountant.

It was in the Department of Labour and National Service that Mary experienced clear discrimination against women for the first time. The department needed women as clerks so they could release the men to go off to war, so they advertised for women as temporary clerks at the male pay rate. Mary applied for one of these jobs but was warned by a friend not to let on she could write shorthand. The department was desperately short of stenographers but female stenographers were paid only four pounds a week while the lowest level male clerk got five pounds a week.

Mary took her friend's advice and didn't let on in interview that she could write shorthand. So she was given a temporary job (while the men were away) as a Grade One Clerk at five pounds a week. Such was the inconsistency in pay practised through discrimination.

After the war Mary had her three children: her first baby, Rosemary, was born in 1947 when she was 27; Wendy was born in 1950; and David in 1953. For the next eight years, while the children were young and she was caring for them, Mary maintained some independence taking in typing at home to earn an income. 'I always had some part-time work I could do at home and so earned some money of my own, with which I could buy what I wanted without having to go on bended knees to get it from my husband.'

Like Lesley Falloon's husband, and most other middle-class men at the time, Mary's husband was embarrassed that anyone should know his wife worked 'for money'. For reasons Mary doesn't quite understand, with the exception of school fees, her husband was very slow to pay the bills. This embarrassed her so she would pay the bills on time with her income.

> When the children were small I bent over backwards to make sure they had the things other

children had. I made all their clothes and most of mine too. I didn't work outside my home until my third child was at kindergarten—then I worked part-time.

Later I understood Dick's attitude was because of the circumstances in which he was left when his father died. His mother had no pension and his only brother was out of work so he had to support them all. He managed to buy a house for his mother. When we bought a house he was keen to get it paid off as soon as he could. He got a loan from the government as a result of his war service—with 35 years to pay the house off at very low interest—but he insisted on paying it off in less than 15 years, which was silly because he could have invested the money at a much higher interest than he was paying on the loan. But he was so terrified of being in debt he was determined to clear it. He didn't discuss things with me, just made the decisions himself and I had to live on what was left. He probably thought I knew nothing about such matters and, looking back, he was probably right.

Marriage to her much older husband did not prove to be what Mary had expected. She and Richard had been incompatible from the outset. He expected deference from her on every matter except the cooking.

Dick wanted to control everything, especially the money. I had imagined that I would have a home of my own which I could run the way I liked, as my stepmother did, but that didn't happen. I rather think that, because his father was a ship's captain and only home on special occasions—when his wife waited on him hand and foot and did only as he wished—Dick imagined it should be like that for him. His mother was a little Welsh country girl—who maybe never even went to school— brought up by her granny after her mother died. Whatever I did, it was never good enough. Dick expected the house to be perfectly tidy by the time he got home and if he found a toy left in the garden, he would bring it to me with a stern disapproving look on his face and say, 'Who left this outside?' Any visitors or children had to be out of the house before Dad got home and the children were too embarrassed to invite other children home because Dad might 'say something' to them.

Mary retained her interest outside the home, staying in secretarial work until 1956 when her youngest child was three. She then got a job with the Electrical Supply and Service Company of Australia as a sales agent and cooking demonstrator selling Supermix (a food vitamiser) door-to-door; this proved to be her liberation. She discovered she was very good at sales. The job gave her an opportunity to demonstrate that she could earn more money than many men at a time when few women worked. Dick disapproved. But Mary shone.

I was paid the same as the chaps for every machine sold. It was a very competitive business and the manager encouraged competition with a prize each month. If a salesperson sold 31 vitamisers, one each day for a month, they got a prize. I set myself to do this, although I only worked three days a week and all of those who had won so far—all men—worked five days a week. I succeeded once; that was enough to prove a point. I controlled the money I earned and Dick resented that.

Mary's confidence grew and she began to develop interests outside the home. Her upbringing and Christian beliefs led to her concerns for the plight of uneducated women. She had been taught to give to the poor, to care for those less well off than she was and to be thankful she was not like them. She could not bear to see people in real distress and her concerns grew as she saw the conditions under which poor women had to live. She used to do 'good works' in Montague Street on the Port Melbourne rail line. The little lanes that ran off Montague were slums, and in one family a woman lived with her five children while expecting another. Mary's friend's mother, who used to run the Crusader meetings in her home in East St Kilda, took the woman to live in her large house for several weeks until she went into hospital to have her sixth child. But the woman had to return to the slum with her new baby and her eldest child was only thirteen. Mary believed the woman had no hope for the future. 'I realised the appalling things that could happen to people when they are not educated and don't know how to avoid pregnancy. Such girls would often finish up with the backyard abortionists.'

It was her daughter Wendy, a student at Monash University in 1969, who encouraged Mary to go to hear the controversial doctor Bertram Wainer speak in the home of ALP members Daphne and Ian Thorne. Wainer was a brave whistleblower who was lifting the lid on an entrenched culture of police corruption involving abortion practices. Mary and Wendy were enthralled with Dr Wainer, who had set up the Progressive Reform Party, and Mary offered to become its minutes secretary: she would later become its full secretary. This was the beginning of a career that led to Mary's advocacy on behalf of women, particularly their health care and workplace equality.

> I don't think the Progressive Reform Party ever got anyone into Parliament but it stirred things up. Bert was attacked by the police because a woman who'd had a backyard abortion somewhere and was bleeding to death was brought into his surgery. She died on the table at the surgery. Bert hadn't operated on her, she was already 'stuffed up', but that set him off campaigning for legalised abortion.
>
> I investigated people who had complaints against the St Kilda police. I remember we interviewed one chap whom they had treated abominably and

three senior policemen finally went to jail. My daughter Rosemary and I wrote it all up. The police would invade the surgeries of qualified people who were carrying out abortions so women would be driven to go to unqualified, unhygienic, backyard abortionists. The police set Bert up and broke into his surgery and prevented him from practising. They wanted to get him because he was advocating for better conditions but also he was finding out that the prostitutes were going to the backyard abortionists recommended by the police, and they probably all had their hands in their pockets. So that was where I got involved.

Mary was 42 when she changed jobs, in 1963, and went to work for a union, the Association of Architects, Engineers, Surveyors and Draughtsmen of Australia (AAESDA). Her duties were to include training as an industrial advocate and supervising the production of a monthly union journal *Blueprint* as the publication manager and subeditor. At last she could draw on her writing skills. By the time she joined the staff of the architects' union Mary had worked as a typist, stenographer, private secretary, door-to-door sales woman and demonstrator. She soon found the unions behaved much the same as everyone else when it came to discriminating against women.

She never did get the industrial advocate training. A young man with no qualifications, except some ALP connections, was brought in, starting on a salary above

Mary's; he eventually became the Federal Secretary of the union.

> *Blueprint* was a typical union journal—as boring as anything. I was not the editor—the Federal Secretary of the union was the editor and he used to supply the editorial. But I did all the proofreading and layout as well as rewriting all the stuff that was sent in. I made it look a lot more attractive but, of course, I got no acknowledgement, financial or otherwise.

By now Mary was learning how to be strategic about winning a point and effecting change in the workplace. She was not going to accept discrimination quietly. Her boss, Graham Walker, who later became Commissioner at the Conciliation and Arbitration Commission, was her mentor.

> I joined the Australian Journalists' Association (AJA) and applied for a salary appropriate to a sub-editor. With the help of the Federal Secretary of the AJA at the time I got what I asked for—a substantial increase over what I'd been getting and—as people used to say—that's good pay for a woman!
>
> They were a comparatively lively union—what you call these days 'left wing'. It was almost all male. They had organisers in various factories and that was when I really started to get interested in women. In the early days I was interested in equality, but not just for women.

As Mary was becoming more assertive in her job she also decided she did not want to stay with Richard any longer and her daughters were encouraging her to leave the marriage after 26 years. She left him in 1967. By then she had also become an agnostic: 'open to evidence, but nothing has convinced me so far.' Two years later, at the urging of her daughter Wendy, she read Betty Friedan's *The Feminine Mystique*.

> I can remember sitting in the office at lunchtime reading this fascinating book. We did just accept that was the way it was. You thought you had to get married because you couldn't earn enough as a woman. Some man was supposed to support you. The working women were mostly lower-class women who worked in factories. When I went out to work, my father and my husband were embarrassed, especially when I was selling supermixers and went around knocking door-to-door.

Along with women throughout the Western world Mary recognised Friedan was articulating her feelings about the dominant sexist ideology which bound women to domestic roles and limited their horizons. This book, along with *The Female Eunuch* and *Damned Whores and God's Police*, helped Mary clarify her thinking. Instinctively she had rebelled against the discrimination which allowed unequal pay for men and women but these books gave her a broader understanding of the social and political structures that kept women housebound and dependent on men.

With her confidence growing, her ability to earn a living confirmed, and her understanding of the basis of discrimination more clearly defined, Mary accepted an invitation to join the Women's Electoral Lobby (WEL). At first, 'very primly', she said, 'I don't believe in women-only organisations.' But when she learned there were three male members: 'a Maori chap, Ian McPhee (the Liberal politician) and one other called Aldo, whom I met again in October 2012 during Seniors' Week, I joined.' At 51 this was Mary's real 'change of life'.

> There were all these women who were younger than I was, and they all had young children. They were your typical women at home, not in paid employment. They were running families, and they were fed up with the way things were going and thought it high time that women had more say in things. Most of them had been to university, which I hadn't. I was just so impressed with how much they knew and the things they did and how they got involved in the abortion issue too. Here at last was a group of knowledgeable, articulate women who were not just whingeing about what was wrong with their lives but who were prepared, willing and able to do something about it.

They were an inspiration to Mary. It was now the early 1970s, the Whitlam era, and time for a change. WEL became active in making politicians accountable for their position on issues affecting women, who made up, after all, half the electorate and were about to make their votes count. As Mary became active in politics she found that women could actually *do* something about changing conditions in society. Such involvement was her forté; she was good at writing submissions, confronting the media, selling ideas and winning people over. She threw herself into the task, busy all the time, and thoroughly enjoyed all the action: she felt alive.

> If anyone had a mandate, Whitlam did, because he told us in advance what he planned to do. Not like now when both the major parties only tell you what they think will win your vote and nothing about the majority of people in Australia. The great thing Whitlam did for me was to give me three years at Melbourne University free of charge; I had been waiting nearly 40 years since I matriculated at the age of 15 for this opportunity.

So in 1974, in her mid-fifties, when the Whitlam Government made tertiary education free for all, Mary went to university to do an Arts degree, majoring in psychology and politics. It would take her until 1986 to complete her degree because throughout that period she worked full time and was kept extremely busy on numerous committees, travelling interstate and sometimes having to miss an exam because of a pressing political issue. But once more Mary's life opened up to another dimension.

She had formally divorced Richard in 1973 and would not find another partner, but he never accepted she was gone from his life.

> He kept trying to win me back but he used the wrong tactics: depriving me of money, then offering to provide me with a lovely new home—complete with him. During his last five or six years I used to go and see him in the various nursing homes where he was and he never gave up—but always on his terms. One nurse told me he was the most demanding patient she had ever had to cope with.

Although Mary missed out on that promised advocacy training from AAESDA a decade earlier, she became an advocate acting on behalf of WEL in 1974 with the national wage case for the minimum wage for women. She was involved in numerous committees designed to help women obtain equality and as 1975—International Women's Year—approached, Mary formed part of a women's committee that asked the Whitlam Government for money to set up a Resource Centre for Working Women.

> We put in a submission for funding to set up a Working Women's Centre (WWC) in Melbourne to advise women on industrial matters and got

$40,000 as a one-off grant. This covered wages for two coordinators and a clerical assistant. Sylvie Shaw, who conceived the idea for the WWC, made it clear that she wanted to be one of the coordinators and Bill Richardson, the Federal Secretary of Australian Council of Salaried and Professional Associations (ACSPA), asked me if I would take the other position. It was a bit of a risk giving up a secure job, where I was well known, for a job that was only guaranteed for a year. However, I had never had any trouble getting work, my three children were more or less off my hands, I was 51 and thought we might have a chance to get something really worthwhile going and I would like to contribute to it.

I think some other people thought I was mad to give up a secure job for pie-in-the-sky. A few thought I was noble. Probably some thought, 'There goes Mary off on another of her crusades.' I don't think I've thought much about what other people might think of me.

This independence of mind is characteristic. She once told an interviewer: 'The more radical elements of the women's movement have often considered me to be fairly wet. But the conservatives think I'm radical. So, in a way, I don't please anyone.'

At the end of the initial year, Mary had managed to cajole money from the unions to continue the work of the WWC, and then from governments: she remained joint coordinator for 10 years. This was the decade when Mary did her most important work on behalf of women.

> At the Working Women's Centre women would come to us with a problem for us to solve and that's exactly what we did. We got to know people and where to go to deal with a problem. Sometimes you could solve it; sometimes you couldn't. Women used to go to the union but of course the unions weren't very good at helping at that early stage; so in 1979 Sylvie Shaw and I produced a resource—a book of papers, mostly written by Sylvie, on women's issues—called *Working Women: Discussion Papers from the Working Women's Centre Melbourne.*
>
> Another thing we did was set up a register of women in non-traditional occupations. We had a speakers' list, and we used to choose women who worked in non-traditional roles to go out to schools and give talks, so the girls could consider becoming apprentices in trades. The Trades Hall eventually took it over and didn't know what to do with it and let it lapse.

In 1979 the Australian Council of Trade Unions (ACTU) took over the WWC. Part of the amalgamation deal was that the WWC would go with them. Bill Kelty, an influential figure in the ACTU, left a memo on Mary's desk suggesting she might retire and act in an advisory capacity, but she informed him she was going to stay until she was 65 as she was entitled to do. 'You should have seen the smile on Kelty's face when I went and told him that I proposed to retire on 8 February 1986, which was my birthday. He put his arm around me and took me to get a coffee from the machine in the office!'

After Mary retired she enjoyed a year full time at Melbourne University to complete her degree. She later became a Member of La Trobe University Council (1983–90) and was Deputy Chancellor in 1989.

Mary remains outspoken about women's issues and inequality. She has given many lectures and talks to schools throughout Victoria, to universities, management seminars, unions, women's organisations and groups, government-sponsored seminars and workshops and has been a regular media commentator in the press and on radio and television. There are three main issues she still cares about passionately: government money that goes to private-health insurance, private superannuation and private education.

> Instead of giving tax concessions which are of far more benefit to the rich than to the rest of us, the federal government should be investing in public education, public health services and a decent retirement pension for everybody. I think that the state should provide free education at a much higher standard for everybody. I think that trying to buy votes with tax concessions is quite wrong.

Mary worries about who will carry the banner

forward and she is looking to younger women to join
her Older Women's Network.

In a way WEL has been too successful. So many of
their most vocal, efficient members are now senior
members of state and federal bureaucracies and
often unable to take a public position on issues of
importance to women. But they have changed the
way the bureaucracy and government work for the
better.

They do have to realise that it will all slip back
again if the young ones don't take it on. I think
Australia has come a long way in my lifetime in
the promotion of women's rights, but all these
achievements are under constant threat. It is
essential that young women study the history of
women's liberation and realise that we must be
vigilant and ever ready to defend what we have won,
not with clenched fists and chanted slogans, but
with reasoned argument and persistence through
the ballot box and through lobbying government
and bureaucracy until we wear them down. I
don't want women to beat men at their own game.
I want women to show men a new way, based on
community action and care for each other.

Joining with other women in efforts to try to
improve life on Earth for all of us is what has given
most meaning to my life.

Today I am slower: life is more stressful in
that I cannot keep up with all that I want to do.
I have daytime naps and seldom take on more

than one major outing or task in one day. Ageing is damn inconvenient, but it is less stressful in that I feel no need to try to keep up with anyone else's expectations. I live mostly on my own but I have friends with whom I share outings and do volunteer work, folk who ring and email me and seem to like to keep in touch. My day runs away with me. I rise at 6.30 to 7am, prepare breakfast, feed the birds, put away last night's washing-up, then go back to bed and read the *Age*. Then I'm up and off to exercise class or whatever. At 4pm I rest and listen to Phillip Adams on the ABC if I am at home. I prepare dinner, which I eat in front of TV—ABC1 or maybe SBS1. I have five books on the go at the moment. The important interests and activities in my life are the Older Women's Network, writing submissions to government, politics, gardening, visiting incarcerated friends, and trying to write memoirs.

There is no especially regular highlight to my week except when my daughter Wendy sometimes comes and stays a night or two. My children are not children, of course; they are 64, 61 and 58 and my grandchildren are 24, 21 and 17. I seldom see them because two live in the USA, three in Western Australia and one between Italy and Point Lonsdale. My second daughter stores a lot of her belongings in my house and when she is in Australia I see her fairly often. They are all very important. I do think about them all the time and I do worry quite a bit about them for various reasons.

What are the reasons Mary has lived a long life?

Genes, strict parenting, which taught me to look after myself, and a lot of luck. I'm lucky I didn't take up smoking until I was in my mid-thirties and never did the drawback. I gave up 30 years later when I had a mini-stroke. I also think my involvement with many interesting women and a few chaps has kept me stimulated. Old people to me are those who accepted what they were told and mostly left someone else to make decisions.

At the end of life it is important to have friends, including family, a secure restful environment and lack of physical pain. I think the most important asset anyone can have is friends.

———————— ◆ ————————

CHAPTER 8

THE
ANAESTHETIST

JOHN TUCKER 1918–

JOHN Tucker has led a joyful, challenging, exciting and satisfying life. He loved being a medical student, a doctor during World War Two, and an anaesthetist for 40 years, and assisting surgeons working throughout South-East Asia. He had practical skills and led a balanced life, enjoying music and carpentry, athletics, tennis and cycling, and he was a devoted husband and family man. Tucker always applied himself, worked hard and his enthusiasm achieved results.

Such a marvellous and fortunate life came to an abrupt halt with the death of his beloved wife Margaret on 14 July 2000, his partner and collaborator for 52 years.

Life lost its appeal for him on that day, but he has carried on, happy to be alive and motivated by his extended family, friends and interests. He has written a memoir of his life and at 94 he continues to attract people. 'I only have to go out onto the street and someone will come and ask, *Can I help you?*'

John Tucker was born exactly a week after Armistice Day ended World War One. His father, Cecil Finn Tucker, was a general practitioner; his mother, Lavina Louise Kelly, an attractive redhead, was a nurse at the Royal Children's Hospital in Melbourne when she met Cecil. They were wed in 1912 and had four children— Margot, Kathleen, Horace and John. 'I had a very happy childhood due to my mother and father, my two sisters and brother and my cousins, called Butler—seven of them—and their friends. We were one big happy family aided by music, tennis and golf. Life was full of nice, happy and interesting people and marvellous music.'

John's mother gave birth at home (which was common at the time), on the corner of Bay and New streets in Brighton. He went to kindergarten for two years at Firbank and remembers skipping into school while his teacher, Miss Hope, played Percy Grainger's 'Country Gardens' on the piano. He would become the school doctor there twenty years later.

Kindergarten was not far but it was uphill; John walked until he was given a tricycle. Then he would hurtle down the hill from school, one day coming to grief and slamming his tricycle into the nearby hotel. He was a lively boy, full of vigour and mischief. He understood right from wrong, although he tossed a rock through a neighbour's open window on the way home from school one day and has felt guilty about it all his life. He and his brother Horace were adventurous, cheeky little boys who tested the parameters of their young lives.

Just how much has changed for us all in the 10 decades John Tucker has lived is evident in his description of life in the suburb where he spent his early years. Brighton was like a village. The tradesmen went door to door delivering their goods—the milkman, the baker, the greengrocer, the butcher and the iceman who carried ice to cool the ice-chest. A hansom cab sat outside the railway station waiting for business, the horse perfectly groomed and the driver in a long black coat and top hat. The majority of households did not have a car, a telephone or a wireless (certainly not a television set): it would be the end of the 1920s before the wireless arrived, making a big difference to entertainment in the home. Today's old have experienced the beginnings of much that we take for granted now—it gives them perspective and a sense of what really matters in living a good life.

In the absence of electronic media, music played an important part in the lives of many families. As a child John aspired to be an actor and a singer as he loved music so much, particularly musical theatre like Rodgers and

Hammerstein or Gilbert and Sullivan. John's parents also enjoyed musicals and took their young son to the theatre to see shows like *The Desert Song, No No Nanette* and *The Merry Widow*. How John loved those musicals. He saw all these shows at least once and learned the words to all the songs. Hearing these musicals throughout his life would often bring him to tears. He always owned a crystal set, and he made his first in about 1930.

There were only four doctors in Brighton at that time. Cecil saw most of his patients in their homes, not in the surgery, and John was occasionally taken on rounds with his father. He loved those rounds, the time spent with his dad, who would teach him the names of all the motor cars on the road. A patient paid 10 shillings and sixpence, or half a guinea, per consultation, which is exactly what John charged years later when he started in general practice in 1950. Back then, a general practitioner did surgery and almost all the obstetrics in the practice as there was not the specialisation there is today.

Following kindergarten John went to Grimwade House at Melbourne Grammar School. The headmaster liked to meet the boys one at a time, to get to know them all well. When asked his name while waiting for his meeting, he replied, 'John.' This created quite a lot of amusement because at Grimwade first names were never used; he was meant to say 'Tucker'. From then on if anyone called him anything but Tucker it would have been Tommy, a nickname deriving from the famous nursery rhyme.

Tucker also enjoyed the pictures. The first he saw, when he was eight and nine were silent movies—Buster Keaton in *The General* and *Rin Tin Tin*, starring the famous German Shepherd. Going to the picture theatre was quite an occasion. Theatres were large, distinctive and grand. At the start of the film a Wurlitzer organ would rise out of the floor with an organist playing it and would disappear again at the end—a fascinating sight for a child.

Young Tucker seemed to get into a lot of fights at school. The boys used to go around in gangs and brawl with one another. Boxing was a sport at Grimwade and anyone not taking part was looked upon as 'a bit of a squib'. Tucker was small but did not lack for courage so for six years he boxed but he hated it. He would front up in the ring to his opponent, who was often twice his size, and take a hiding, but, as was true throughout his life, his spirit was never smashed.

In his second year at Grimwade, Tucker's parents went overseas and he and his brother Horace became boarders. The bullying culture that still survives in many schools was prevalent then. Tucker wore boots which had big loops at the back with which to pull them on. One Sunday afternoon some of the bigger boys put a rope through these loops and started to drag him around the oval. When his trousers were coming up around his neck Horace rushed onto the field to his brother's aid but the boys beat him up too: it was a not a good day for the Tuckers.

Horace, too, was regarded as a troublemaker for the mischief he got into. One weekend he and his friend Ted Oakley made a toy cannon with a bit of metal tubing, which they blocked at one end and stuffed pellets and gunpowder made out of match heads in the other. They put some wheat on the lawn and put a kerosene tin either side of the grain and waited for a chook to come and eat the wheat. Then they put a match to the cannon. The cannon blew up, the chook was unharmed, and Oakley's parents came rushing out to find Ted and Horace flat out on the lawn. Horace's hearing was affected for some time and Ted had damaged fingers, but they survived the misadventure.

Tucker did not learn the lesson. He and a friend, Bertie Southwell, set fire to a tree in the Botanic Gardens to see if cobwebs would burn. Then he and his friend Peter Grant-Hay burned down a marquee set up for a big party when Tucker threw crackers on it. They were sent to bed early and Tucker doesn't remember paying any more visits to the Grant-Hays' homestead.

In school they were taught times tables by a teacher who would shout out the sum and point at a boy who had to answer without pause. If you paused you had to come back to school on Saturday. Tucker still answers instantly if someone says 'seven sixes'. Each night they were given spelling to learn for the next day and if anyone got more than two mistakes they would be caned. In 1929 Tucker was caned almost every day. His mother got rather upset about the caning so she lined his trousers with leather from her husband's driving gloves.

Tucker was a practical child who loved building things. In 1929 the family went to live in a lovely old home set back on almost an acre of land at 316 St Kilda Street, Brighton. There was a large garden and big trees to climb; in front was a grass tennis court. He thinks his father paid £6000 for the place, a lot of money at the time. Cecil was a keen gardener and was fond of birds, but it was John who built the first aviary.

Horace and Tucker moved to the senior school at Melbourne Grammar. Tucker set himself two goals in his final year. One was to run a mile for the school in the combined sports and the other was to matriculate. He was athletic and he was fast. He won his house mile quite easily but circumstances kept him out of representing his school at the combined sports. It was one of the great disappointments of his life. But he did matriculate. What was he going to do with his life?

Tucker had always said he was going to do medicine but his father thought he should follow his practical and outdoor interests. He believed that John was temperamentally unsuited to medicine. But when Tucker found out that 15 or more people from Melbourne Grammar intended to do medicine and 10 of them were doctors' sons, he went back to his father and insisted he wanted to do medicine. His father agreed. Most of Tucker's attempts to achieve anything in those days were done to please his father, who always took an interest in him, even back in his younger days, when he would make model aeroplanes. 'He would quite often drive me out to the paddock and watch me flying them.'

One hundred and seventy people started medicine in 1937 and 70 failed first year. If you didn't work hard you fell by the wayside quickly. Tucker applied himself to study while continuing to play sport; it was a good mix. In second year he cemented friendships in the anatomy lab: students spent every morning for two years carving up cadavers. It was a great meeting place and lifelong relationships were formed. Tucker was captain of the university hockey team and was awarded a full hockey blue, recognising his performance at the highest level.

By Tucker's third year World War Two was underway and it was not unusual for those not in uniform to be asked why they were not at war. Tucker took a job in a soap factory for two months, working 40 hours a week, and realised what a sheltered life he had lived. He was paid 37 shillings and sixpence a week and received a social education as well as an insight into work life. Later he was paid the same amount as a junior resident doctor at the Alfred Hospital.

Most doctors in training felt self-conscious that they were not in one of the services. They were sent to army training camp over Christmas, but the medical unit of the Melbourne University Rifles was looked on as a bit of a joke. As a result of the war, final exams were moved forward from year's end to May 1942. This added pressure, as the same amount of work had to be covered. Tucker qualified among 110 graduates in total. He felt a loss, leaving his time as a student behind: they had been enjoyable years. But he was a long way from being qualified to treat patients independently as a doctor.

> Doctors who have completed the medical course are quite unprepared to practise medicine. They have learned a tremendous amount of theory but still have a lot more to learn. In peacetime they spend one to three years as resident doctors working under supervision in a hospital before going into private practice and you require at least another five years to qualify in a specialty. Life as a junior resident was the most enjoyable year of my whole medical life. Never at any time in your life do you learn so much each day as you do as a junior resident. You really begin to feel you are becoming a doctor.
>
> There being a war on, we all went to the various public hospitals as junior residents for nine months to a year and then into the services. There were a few people each year who for some reason or other refused to join up, which I always thought was a very brave thing to do, but most of us were of the age where we just couldn't wait to get into it.

Tucker chose to go into the army. Being a doctor, he was given the rank of captain but was sent to an army school for a four-week crash course on how to be a captain. At the end of officer school they were sent to a unit. Tucker was sent with two friends to the 2/4th Australian Field Ambulance, which was on the Atherton Tableland. His reputation as an athlete went with him. In May 1943, after he had just joined the unit as medical officer (MO), he ran the last lap for the infantry battalion inter-unit sports day. Starting third and finishing first, he wore off all the skin from the pads of his toes on his bare feet. For the next week he had to walk about the unit on his heels.

He found the action he had been looking for in New Guinea, as part of the assault on Lae, where 'the medical unit set up a small hospital in an old mission building at Nadzab'. Tucker was then sent to join the 2/10th battalion as the Regimental Medical Officer (RMO).

> This was a fine group of 800 men who had been training and fighting for over four years. It was a delight and a privilege to be with them.
>
> On July 1, 1945 I was involved in an amphibious landing at Balikpapan, Borneo. We were dropped out in the water and not on the beach. One poor fellow had a heavy mortar base plate strapped to his back and disappeared below the surface, not to be seen again. I took my unit to the top of the hill, as directed. The town was taken with only moderate

casualties and nearly half of those were the result of bombs which fell on the Headquarter Company dropped from planes from an American aircraft carrier. Not realising we had taken Hill 87, they thought we were Japanese. I remember standing on Hill 87 and watching these aircraft, which we had decided rightly were ours, when suddenly we saw bombs falling from them and dived for cover. They landed all around the Regimental Aid Post. It was a tragedy and very sad as they killed and wounded quite a few members of the battalion, all of whom I knew well. I was very busy from then on and eventually had to send dead and wounded back in the same vehicles, something we'd tried to avoid.

Peace came suddenly as far as we were concerned. We had heard that someone had split the atom and that it was possible to make a bomb so powerful that it could wipe out whole cities, but of course 'it would not be used'.

The first I knew of Japan's surrender was a sudden outburst of rifle fire and grenades a mile or so from our camp and we naturally thought the Japs must have launched an attack on the town. But we soon learned that it was the Americans celebrating the end of the war. I gather in some areas they went so completely mad that many troops were wounded and some killed. We had quite a pleasant party ourselves but managed to do it without firing a shot.

Tucker had been away for more than three years. All he wanted to do was get on with being a doctor. Still in the military, he was appointed Admitting Officer at the Heidelberg Military Hospital and was later in charge of the surgical ward—'a marvellous job', he thought. It meant he saw every soldier returning from overseas, assessed his state of health and referred him for investigation and treatment. The prisoners of war were all returning during Tucker's time on admissions.

> A lot of them came back through Bangkok and quite a number of them acquired venereal disease there, which was rather sad as these people were returning home to their families after a long and unpleasant absence. I was very impressed with the way this difficult situation was handled by the army. I was told to refer any such case to a special hospital. There they were treated with penicillin, which only took about a week and the men were allowed to go home. Their families were not told of their arrival until they had been pronounced cured, which saved a great deal of heartache.
>
> I was demobilised in July 1946 and had decided I wanted to become a surgeon.

At the beginning of 1947 Tucker sat for the first part of the Master of Surgery and passed. He then spent a year as a Junior Resident MO at the Royal Children's Hospital as an associate attached to a senior surgeon. He had been qualified as a doctor for 10 years by now and it would be another three to four years before he could sit for the second part of the surgical degree. He was having doubts about whether he should be doing surgery at all. These doubts were strengthened because he had fallen deeply in love with Margaret Wallace. It wasn't medicine that attracted Margaret to John: she thought he was a farmer because his hands were so rough from spending so much time in his beloved workshop making things.

At 30 John sat for his surgery fellowship exam in May 1949 and did not pass; he then made what he considered to be the worst decision of his life and the most sensible decision of his life. He decided to go into partnership in general practice and to marry Margaret.

He spent two years in general practice but was never completely happy. He then made the decision to become an anaesthetist, so he continued with study, being paid £200 a year. Margaret took on piano teaching to supplement their income and they lived very simply. He qualified as a Fellow of the Faculty of Anaesthetics of the Australian College of Surgeons in February 1952. For the next 40 years John Tucker worked as an anaesthetist, content in his chosen profession.

On six occasions he travelled through the developing countries of Asia and South-East Asia assisting surgeons under the Colombo Plan. This plan, formed after World War Two, was designed to help developing countries. The Minister for Foreign Affairs (R.G. Casey) decided that Australia would send senior medical personnel to these countries to teach medical techniques. Tucker was asked to go with a surgeon, Sir Benjamin Rank, to India, which meant he was away for several months without pay operating on children with cleft palates. This experience was one of the highlights of his life.

> In Calcutta the enthusiastic Hindu Indian doctors crowded into the theatre each day and gathered around the patient, some balancing on chairs, some even on ladders, and it was difficult to get a look at the poor patient. I had to be content with one hand from which I could tell the colour of the patient and take the pulse. I could hear the breathing through a stethoscope on a long tube. If Rank wasn't happy with the colour of the patient I would have to burrow my way through the onlookers until I could see the whole patient, see the breathing and make a general assessment. On one occasion one of the Indian doctors slipped from the ladder on which he was standing precariously and landed on top of Rank, causing him to make a large incision in a child's palette. I heaved a sigh of relief and gratitude each day when, eventually, we did the last case without serious mishap. I felt we were all living dangerously— particularly the patients. We operated at Calcutta, Delhi, Nagpur, Hyderabad, Madura, Madras and Colombo, staying about three weeks in each place and doing five or six cases each day.

It was stressful work; there was constant fear of tragedy, working under difficult conditions with a language problem. But Casey was so pleased that he decided medical staff should make annual visits to the least developed countries, so Pakistan was next in December 1955.

In 1963 Tucker accompanied John Bignell, chief eye surgeon at the Royal Melbourne Hospital, and four other eye surgeons, to India, where blindness is common due to the prevalence of cataract disease. In Kota a rich man had arranged for hundreds of blind people to gather at his village under his financial care.

> There was no hospital in the town, no medical facilities of any kind, so we had to improvise using a large cowshed for an operating theatre. The surgeon had brought twelve sets of surgical instruments with him, which were sterilised in a half drum filled with water and boiled over an open fire. Each patient was covered in a long strip of sterile paper about six feet by three feet with a hole torn for the operation. In this simple way, with no overheads, hundreds of patients underwent surgery.
>
> I was amazed how well the cases did considering the conditions. We did a 'ward' round each day and in general the patients were very happy lying there on the ground and there were almost no complications. We encountered criticism back in Australia for operating under such conditions but I was of the opinion that it was a better option for all those patients, seeing the alternative was remaining blind.

In 1964 Tucker accompanied two surgeons on a three-and-a-half-month goodwill tour of South-East Asia. He suffered from chronic diarrhoea for more than a year after that visit, along with a general feeling of tiredness, chronic conjunctivitis and weight loss. He was treated for amoebic dysentery but continued his work in Vietnam, Bangkok, Singapore, Kuala Lumpur and Jakarta. In total he completed 18 months of honorary overseas work as an anaesthetist.

At home, life with Margaret was everything Tucker hoped it would be. They had gone to live at 2 Kembla Street, Hawthorn, in 1955 and lived there for 35 very happy years. They had two sons and one daughter— Robert, Andrew and Christine—and ensured the children led active physical lives, taking the three kids up to Mount Buller each year to ski. As well as his sporting interests, Tucker loved to build all types of things in his workshop.

> I was never as happy as when I was constructing something, and Margaret was never as happy as when I'd at last finished whatever it was. I converted an old building in the backyard into a cottage and over the years we had some very different personalities and good company stay in this cottage.
>
> Margaret used it as a place to help people. One good example was Pip, a girl of 15 who wrote to the *Age* saying she needed somewhere to live and Margaret said 'come to me'. The girl, we found later,

had given birth at 14, had an alcoholic mother and absent father. She became a member of our family and we were able to help her go on to become a nurse and later an ordained Anglican minister.

Margaret so often converted Tucker's dreams into reality. She helped him organise a drive around Australia with the family in 1962. When Tucker got an urge to walk the Kokoda Trail and told Margaret about this over a gin and tonic, she contacted the army and got maps. With their son Andy, they walked the track in 1968. Tucker believes Margaret may have been the first white woman to walk the full length of the track. They walked in New Zealand, the Himalayas, England, Scotland and Wales—the Pennines and the Cotswolds—and in the United States.

At Kembla Street, Tucker constructed a tennis court and played regularly. Around 1967, when water restrictions became necessary, he changed his court to en tout cas and installed lights. At 7pm every Wednesday and Thursday evening he had a fixed date with three friends to play tennis. He was still playing tennis when he was 86. The group was run by Sir Thomas Webb, a man with wide-ranging interests in shipping and industrial affairs, who was a former Chairman of the Commercial Bank of Australia (CBA). He played tennis until the week he died at age 97. Phillip Law, the Antarctic scientist, and Peter Isaacson were still playing tennis at 92. They called themselves 'the awesome foursome'. Tucker played tennis for 60 years before he began going to AFL matches with a friend instead.

In 1983, on the occasion of his 65th birthday, his friend D.W. Rogers wrote a poem about Tucker's tennis and tenacity:

Is There Life After Tennis?
A keen and wiry little man
Built more like Kermit than Tarzan,
Tucker interrupts athletics
With daytime stints of anaesthetics
Then home to Kembla's tennis court
Where playing like a man distraught,
He tenders his profound regrets
For only playing seven sets...
I think that I will never see
John Tucker in a cemetery,
Unless some way has then been found
Of playing tennis underground.

Matters of the mind were not neglected, despite all the sport. The Tucker Dining Club inaugural meeting was held on 20 June 1977, to plan several dinners a year, each with a member or guest giving a short talk on a topical subject to be followed by a discussion. It was a sign of the times that several members were against the idea of inviting wives as members. They resolved that wives would be asked as guests for the first two dinners. In retrospect, Tucker finds it very hard to believe that they all agreed to that. The 'girls' came to the first two and all meetings from then on—they met 57 times in total.

Tucker's energy and productivity were extraordinary throughout his life, and he began to fancy himself as a farmer. He knew nothing about farming but would imagine himself on Sundays out on a tractor or mustering sheep on horseback.

He and Margaret bought 400 acres of land at Caveat, about 150 kilometres from Melbourne. Margaret acquired 20 Hereford heifers and a thoroughbred bull which she called Brodribb, but eventually she fell in love with growing blueberries. Within three years they had good berries, which Margaret would drive to the market. She became an advisor for new growers and she helped start 'pretty well everyone in the business'. This was another stage of reinvention for both partners in a life of interesting challenges.

> I retired in 1990. Most hospitals like an anaesthetist to retire at 70 years and I retired when I was 72. I was very much against it but later really enjoyed retirement and was glad that I had. Margaret said, 'You have done all the work so far, now it is my turn. I will do my best to make some money.' She was being hard on herself as she had run the girl guides and introduced blueberries.

They sold Caveat and bought at Drysdale, a property they named Tuckerberry Hill. When they took it over it was just a 20-hectare paddock full of phalaris. They had a dam built, planted hundreds of trees and four hectares of blueberries, and installed a large pump at the dam and an irrigation system.

Later they decided to build a house at Drysdale and it was bad news for Margaret when Tucker decided to do most of the construction himself. He was a man of great energy and determination, but it took him six years to get the house to the stage where they could move in. Most weekends and holidays Tucker forsook his tennis and came to Drysdale to work on the house. The blueberries would start to ripen in December and Margaret opened the orchard to the public on Boxing Day. In 2000 she was awarded an OAM in the New Year's Honours for bringing blueberries into Australia.

Margaret died of leukaemia on 14 July 2000, aged 73, after 52 years of marriage.

> I must say, life has completely lost its appeal and, for that matter, its purpose and I don't have much interest in carrying on, but I have been greatly assisted by my children and grandchildren and some of my closer friends to whom I am very grateful. Our relationship was near perfect in every way...I am thankful for the good fortune and luck that I've had, but I'm sad and lonely. Laughter used to be a very big part of my life and possibly the reason I had lived so long, but since Margaret died 13 years ago I can't find much to laugh about,

just occasionally. I have had a marvellous and fortunate life but it's no good now. I believe others think I am a bit strange but they don't seem to have any idea what I go through.

In July 2005 Tucker went to live at a retirement home, the Hawthorn Grange, along with 54 old ladies and five old gentlemen. I have been told some of the ladies were very pleased to see him. His experience of what is often derided as an 'old folks' home' is not negative except for mealtimes, when he is required to sit with people who have lost the capacity for conversation.

I have quite a nice room and bathroom and three good meals a day if I happen to be there at the time. It is quite sad to see many of the fellow residents, particularly those who cannot see to read, just sit there for hours each day, usually by themselves, waiting for God, as it is said.

Seeing people and reading are important activities in my life now I have not got the pleasure from my work. A good book is a highlight. I read four to five hours per day. The last book I read was by Mark Twain and I like reading scientific books. I visit people and doctors each day and fill in the rest of the time reading or occasionally writing something on the computer. I watch the seven o'clock news on the ABC followed by the 7.30 which I feel, like most TV shows, is deteriorating.

It is very important to have interests outside work for a happy retirement and these should be developed during your life as it is difficult to develop interests late in life. I have tried to keep up sport, mainly bowls, reading, seeing people, making things, I love carpentry.

At 94 my lack of sporting ability, my deafness, my poor eyesight, my forgetfulness and inability to write legibly are frustrating, but the hardships I have could be worse. I try to take life as it comes.

The four good old friends I have left are invaluable; I play bowls with them. I did have a lot—there were 190 at my 90th birthday—but most have died. I have a few friends in their seventies and enjoy them. Time goes quickly; as someone said, you feel you are rushing toward death. I am often lonely. I don't want to live by myself; I would like to have a partner but have not found one. I wish I had ways of being a help to others but I'm not good at it. I must keep trying; it's the way to happiness.

I didn't expect to live so long. People ask me why I have lived so long. I believe it is because I have taken a huge amount of exercise; I have not eaten a great deal; I was very happily married. Most people include the role of the medical profession but I can't think of any time they have saved my life yet. Perhaps they may get an opportunity soon.

What advice would I hand on? To do your best in everything that you do and to live a life which you and others can respect. I have tried to have a clear conscience, which is the most valuable thing for me. I could list the importance of honesty, unselfishness, loyalty, helping others—I learned these things from Margaret—making yourself interesting, forgiveness.

Euthanasia is not for me. I considered it 13 years ago but a friend gave me a lecture; it is a squib's way out, it is selfish. I morally supported a good friend in his death as he gave me very good reasons why he should end his life and he did it very well for everybody.

Tucker has gained most satisfaction in life through his family, work and interests. The word he uses most often to describe his life is joy.

His mobile phone carries the voice-mail message: 'Leave a number and I will get back to you; by George, I will.'

CHAPTER 9

THE RELUCTANT MAYORESS

FLORA NOYCE 1921–

FLORA Noyce is the daughter of pioneering farmers who settled in the remote and barren Mallee country of northwestern Victoria. She grew up in the harshest of drought conditions during the Great Depression. Her family survived and the experience of such hardship taught Flora the value of work and persistence. She has spent her life in the service of others, supporting her husband, her family and her community. She is a vital, energetic human being who has always put others before herself and done for them as she would hope they may do for her. She has known tragedy, losing two sons, but has demonstrated the courage and resilience that underpin her life. She remains an optimist who has had much good fortune. People tell Flora she is marvellous. At 91 she hopes to reach old age: 'I hope I get there. I think I must be old as I am older than almost everyone I know.'

Flora Noel Weir was born on Christmas Day 1921 and her mother named her Noel in celebration. She grew up, living with her parents Arthur and Elsie and her two brothers in the remote Mallee scrub, in an area called the Millewa, which had been newly opened for wheat farming in 1923. The hardships were many for these early pioneers and life for their children was circumscribed by the harsh environment. Flora was shaped by these austere times. As she rode her horse in the arid scrub she had time to herself to think about what she would do when she grew up. 'My world was so small, I thought most people in the world would have to be farmers or farmers' wives and farm workers.'

Flora went to a one-teacher school. She thought she would like to become a teacher and to learn singing like her mother. But, 'whatever choice I would *like* to make, I thought I could never make that choice, because I knew nothing of high schools, university or the wider world.'

Flora was the first child and the only girl. Her father was the son of an Irish immigrant who farmed on rugged country at Elmhurst, near Ararat. When the government announced land would be opened up in northern Victoria, Arthur and his new wife Elsie saw an opportunity. This initiative was part of a government scheme to entice returned servicemen from World War One to settle Australia's inhospitable interior. The hope was that small farm holdings would bring diversified farming and community life to remote areas. Until the 1920s, northwest Mallee was one of the few areas of the state still without intensive settlement.

Arthur and Horace, his brother, applied successfully for a lease after riding their bikes 80 miles from Elmhurst to St Arnaud to be interviewed. Arthur moved to Merrinee (about 35 'very long miles' from Mildura) to clear the dense scrub, fence the leased property of 640 acres, sink a dam and build stables for horses. Towards the end of 1924, when Flora was two, the family settled on the property in a small four-room house which had been transported from Red Cliffs. The Weirs came with great energy and optimism but life was tough. Their house was first located too far from the dam to get water so had to be moved: they had no telephone or nearby railway.

Settling new families in the Millewa required massive government spending on roads and railways, irrigation schemes, schools for each town and a district hospital built at Werrimull. The railway line reached Werrimull from Red Cliffs in 1923. Power and telecommunications were not available until the 1940s.

The Millewa settlements were structured with townships every six miles which included a station master's house and a general store. The scheme encouraged the farming sector to grow grain. At first the properties were only two deep, close to the railway so it would be easy to travel with bagged wheat on wagons. There were no branch lines in the 1920s.

Water was the most vital need to be met. Lock 9, completed in 1926, was built over three years on the Murray River to assist the servicing of water to the Millewa. This lock is 24.6 metres above sea level, allowing water to flow into a dry natural depression, Lake Cullulleraine, which prior to 1923 only filled when the river was in high flood. From the lake water was pumped to an extensive array of channels but farmers had to dig their own in the red sandy soil without concrete or pipes and maintain their channelling in the face of windstorms which blew away the topsoil and dumped silt. Not surprisingly, little of the water pumped from the river actually got through to the farmers; in fact, more than 98 per cent was lost due to evaporation and seepage.

The Weirs relied on rainwater tanks for drinking water, while domestic water had to be carried to the house. And rain in the Millewa averaged only 9 inches (225 millimetres) a year for the first 20 years of settlement; in the drought years rainfall was as low as four inches. Before the completion of Lock 9, water would be transported by rail in water tanks and then squirted into long, shallow, unlined holes dug in the ground at the railway station. When the water arrived, the dogs would dive in for a swim and the farmers rushed to scoop out their share before it soaked into the sandy surface. With this life experience Flora has always understood the value of water, retaining the habit of collecting the shower water before it runs hot and using it for washing, a practice now encouraged by environmentalists.

During her first year at school she would walk to a point where another family picked her up to take her to the school where there were 20–30 students of all ages. Later she drove her brothers in the family gig. The family owned a piano and her mother, who was a trained singer, led singalongs with visitors from around the district. This was the way families made social contact and entertained in rural Australia.

There is an energy that comes from hard work and isolation and the people who had cleared the Mallee scrub, dug irrigation channels, and made their own entertainment were a self-reliant and innovative group. A man, his wife and children on a farming lot were a unit. In surviving hardship they built a way of life which had meaning and worth.

The Great Depression in the decade following the 1929 crash crushed many farmers. Below average rainfalls led to low yields, and by the end of the 1930s, over 60 per cent of settlers had left their farms, defeated by isolation, hardship, drought, rabbits and falling commodity prices. Much of the land being opened up simply could not sustain intensive farming.

Australia was hit harder by the Great Depression

than most countries because of our reliance on primary produce and borrowings from British banks which called in their debts. By 1931 a third of Australians were unemployed. When economic recovery began to take effect, war, drought and dust storms followed, with Australia enduring a severe 10-year drought from 1937.

Farmers like Arthur Weir, who had some prior experience of farming, survived by wresting a living from the land with courage, hard work, stoic perseverance and the support of an equally hard-working, resourceful and hospitable wife. The family depended on income from dairy cows. The Weirs separated the milk and twice a week the separated cream was sent by train to the Mildura butter factory.

Their children grew up carrying part of the load, absorbing the work ethic, the community spirit and the values of 'countrymindedness', to borrow Don Aitken's term. They are the values that Flora epitomises. Although they were hard years for her family, Flora remembers them as happy times for her and the other children in the district.

Her mother had grown up in a well-to-do family in Hawthorn. When she decided to marry Arthur Weir she knew she would live a very different, more rugged life as a farmer's wife, proving to her family she could succeed in a difficult rural environment. She became a model to her daughter.

Flora attended school until Year 8 when Merit

Certificates were awarded. Her parents wanted her to receive further education, but to be educated beyond Merit Certificate she had to leave Merrinee. So she was sent to live with three maiden aunts in Avoca when she was 14. (Her eldest brother was sent to Mildura High School as a boarder.) From Avoca, Flora could catch the school bus to nearby Maryborough Technical School. After her one-teacher school Flora was panic-stricken when she was confronted by 300 students at Maryborough Tech, but she settled in and over the next two years learned the skills expected of her: sewing, singing and playing music. She would walk to her paternal grandma's house for piano practice and lessons on Saturday mornings. She obtained her Intermediate Certificate in 1936 and then returned to Merrinee to help her mother run the household.

Flora's mother was left some money by her parents in 1938 and this was to help change their prospects. The Weirs decided to buy a dairy farm on the outskirts of Mildura, still a small, remote town based on an irrigation settlement. The Weirs sold most of their milk to the dairy in Mildura but heated and separated the milk they could not sell to make butter under their own label, Weir Butter.

As his confidence grew, Arthur decided to start his own milk round. It was late 1939 and Flora, then 18, was in her first paid job at the Mildura Ozone Picture Theatre in the ticket box. (My maternal grandfather worked on the door in the evening taking tickets.) Her job was short-lived. In December 1940 Flora's eldest brother Mervyn was called up. As he had not been granted exemption to work in the dairy, Flora had to stop her job at the Ozone Theatre to work with her father and younger brother Bruce.

She would rise at 3.30am with her father and brother to eat a bowl of cereal in a cold kitchen before they milked 24 cows by hand. As 'the worst milker of the lot', she claims she was given all 'the easiest cows' to milk. The animals were well trained and would walk into their own bails, allowing a leg to be tied back to let the milker reach the full udder. When the job was completed the milkers would go back into the house for 'a good wash and a cooked breakfast'. The milk was then water-cooled and poured into 12-gallon cans to be loaded onto two milk carts for delivery. While Flora and her brother had breakfast, her father yoked up the horses to the milk carts.

Milk delivery would often begin in the dark. The horses were trained to move from house to house with a single word: 'Giddup'. Flora had a dappled horse called Toy, which she loved, but the horse must have been 'sanded' and its legs were stiff. 'Unlike rabbits, horses' teeth are made to munch on long grass; however, during the drought years when there was very little long grass to be had the horses had to "chomp" as low as possible, which meant some sand was taken in. This caused pain and stomach upsets and would lead to the hind legs of the horse stiffening.'

'Sanding' caused problems to cart horses like Toy, who worked at a trot. To Flora's distress her pony would sometimes trip on the unsealed roads even though she was shod regularly and her hooves kept trimmed. When Toy stumbled and fell out of her traces it frightened Flora but she learned to deal with it.

Flora's social life was limited to the weekly dance at the Working Man's Club, where she went with her brother Bruce. There, one night in May 1943, she met Neil Noyce, an airforce man on leave from Darwin. Flora had never had, nor had she ever wanted, a boyfriend, but she fell in love at the age of 22 with the man who would be by her side for the next 66 years. The dairy was leased the year Flora met Neil and the family moved to an attractive, large house in Thirteenth Street closer to the centre of Mildura.

Neil was welcomed by the family and often came to Flora's home until he was posted to Melbourne. Flora wanted to go with him so they became engaged on 9 December 1943. She went to Melbourne in January 1944 and got a clerical job with the Commonwealth Aircraft Corporation at Fisherman's Bend, noting aircraft parts coming in, labelling them and sending them out. It was paperwork but she was paid a wage, something she never received at the dairy. Flora rented a bungalow in a backyard in St Kilda with a veranda enclosing a stove and table, and she and Neil would see each other every evening. He lived in the Air Force Barracks at Port Melbourne.

They were both very sure about what they wanted for the future and they flew back to Mildura to marry on 1 July 1944. Their first son, Phillip, was born in April 1945 and Neil was discharged from the RAAF in 1946.

The couple decided to settle in Mildura, where Neil had grown up and Flora's parents had bought a retail dairy, in Ninth Street. Her mother had also bought three houses, which had been transported from the Millewa, and Flora and Neil bought one of them, paying half the cost of the £650 house with the deferred pay that Neil received on discharge. Neil's first job in Mildura was to build a picket fence around the dairy for Flora's father. He began to build up his own joinery business.

The couple managed to settle in their house in Thirteenth Street three weeks before their second son, Ian, was born but the shine was taken off their new home when Flora unpacked the tea chests storing Phillip's baby clothes to find mice had been at work. Not only had the mice chewed many of the knitted baby clothes but they were breeding their own babies, which were hairless and still had their eyes closed. Flora was horrified.

Flora and Neil worked hard and, as her parents had, they prospered. Flora had six tobacco tins in which she allocated her weekly allowance to cover costs and buy new things; they grew their own vegetables. A third son and a daughter came along. Flora cleaned, baked, sewed, gardened, cared for the family and was Neil's confidante. The business expanded: he was soon employing four people and he bought a large block to build a workshop away from the house. He built a new home on Sandilong Avenue and the family moved the day before Christmas in 1953. They were very happy.

Neil was community-minded and joined the Returned Soldiers' League, the RSL, and helped to update their old rooms. As he was becoming a successful businessman, the RSL asked Neil to stand for membership of the Mildura City Council. It was a shock to Flora. She was 34: her daughter Glenda was four and their eldest boy was 11. She did not want to stand in Neil's way but the thought of mixing with the city councillors and playing a role she did not feel qualified to assume caused her anguish.

Flora's father Arthur was by now a very successful businessman and a city councillor. He had come a long way from the young man who cycled to St Arnaud to apply for a lease to settle in Merrinee; all his hard work had paid off. Elsie had adapted well to the role of councillor's wife. But unlike her mother, Flora was most uncomfortable with the idea. Despite her strength of character Flora lacked social confidence.

Membership of Council was not supposed to involve expense but 'it ruddy well did'. Flora could not afford to have her hair done every week, as the other councillors' wives did, and she could not afford the smart clothes expected; she often made her own. Civic receptions were always held at 5pm, a very inconvenient time for four hungry young children. But Flora agreed for Neil's sake that she would play the role to the best of her ability, and from the outset took a strong interest in council issues. She would not go to bed until Neil came home from meetings as there was always so much to talk about.

In time, Neil was approached to stand for mayor. He wanted to stand but he knew how difficult this would be for Flora. Once again, after much soul-searching, she agreed to support him as mayor and Neil was very grateful.

Mildura society was built around a male hierarchy which was defined by the clubs which men joined. Wives fitted in where their husbands 'belonged'. There was the Mildura Club, whose members were the professional men of the town and the monied class. The 'blockies', the land owners, were members of the Settlers Club, and the 'workers' joined the Working Man's Club, which boasted the longest bar in the Southern Hemisphere. Women knew their place on the social ladder and those at the top did their part to maintain the hierarchy. Neil did not belong to the Mildura establishment—those leaders in professions who effectively ran the town—and it was never Flora's ambition for him to join this group. In a small town like Mildura, with its social pretensions, there were those who looked down on a builder and his wife.

Her fears were borne out when twice she was snubbed during Neil's term as mayor. She was also given gratuitous advice from the wife of another councillor, a highly opinionated, confident woman more than a decade older, who 'was a bit of a load to carry. She thought she was assisting me but I didn't want to be assisted.'

In fact, Flora was more independent and more involved than most of the professional older husbands had allowed their wives to be. Things were changing, but only gradually for women in Mildura, and Flora was part of a new wave. She did not think of herself that way but she provided Neil with insights into the world he was operating in by letting him know the views of the women she mixed with, who were taking a more active interest in the politics of the community than women had in the past.

For the first time at mayoral functions Flora and Neil would stand at the door of a reception and personally greet guests on their arrival. On one occasion a woman walked past 'with her nose in the air'. Flora found this hurtful but carried on in her own style. Mayoral obligations included opening school fetes, attending fairs, garden parties, at-homes and civic receptions: it was a demanding role. Flora hated the at-homes, held annually by all the churches and the school mothers' clubs. Flora served three terms as mayoress (1963–64,

1964–65 and 1970–71) and in the end she was an old hand, wearing 'reasonable outfits' that gave her confidence in the public eye. Throughout those years she ran her family, made her clothes, milked a cow twice a day, and made seven pounds of butter a week. Her two eldest sons looked after 400 chooks in a shed Neil had built. On Sunday nights there was always 'a spread to behold', with cakes and pavlovas covered in lashings of beautiful thick dairy cream, all baked by Flora in her Rayburn wood stove.

Although they were personally satisfying years for Neil, they were challenging. Along with the demands of public life he employed an average of 10 to 16 men in his business and did the quotes for all building works they undertook. Flora was his support in all matters but she tended to undervalue her role. Others did not: her view of herself was out of step with the way others saw her.

My parents became friends with Flora and Neil. My father was on the city council for 18 years and worked with Neil in a collaborative partnership. My father Reg, who was a champion at getting things done, was Chairman of Finance, and Neil was Chairman of Works. The two needed to work together for projects to be successful but they shared in the public criticism that results when visionaries rattle the cages. Small-town politics were particularly vicious in Mildura as different interest groups clashed over plans to build an art gallery and theatre for the performing arts. Some councillors were interested in developing the community, others were motivated by personal ambition and populist politics, getting their satisfaction by trying to prevent change. This mix made for tension.

My mother Eva, like Flora, became the mayoress of Mildura for two terms in the early 1950s. Eva had a remarkably similar upbringing to Flora's and also had to overcome a lack of education and confidence to take on a public role, which, like Flora, she did with aplomb. Eva viewed Flora with affection and respect, but the difference between them was that my mother was from an earlier generation with less independence and opportunity to offer her opinions on local politics. Reg regarded his business, including council business, as the business of men. Flora and Neil discussed ideas. He took her advice seriously.

The wives were often brought together by the mutual business interests of their husbands and Eva liked Flora's direct, friendly and sincere style. I appreciated Flora's respect for my mother and thought her similar to Hazel Hawke: people warmed to her because she had no pretensions and seemed genuinely to like them. She did not enjoy the politics and the nastiness, but she understood they came with the job, especially if you were a councillor wanting to get things done.

On 13 July 1968, Neil and Flora were at an official function. They were called away by the police at 11pm to learn that their son Richard had been killed in a

car accident. They had left him at home with his sister
Glenda watching television and believed him safely in
bed. His friend had come by and suggested a drive in his
new sports car. The Noyce family was changed forever
by this accident; Richard was only 18 years old. Still in
the public eye, Flora and Neil felt obliged to go on. Flora
recalls:

> Following Richard's death I did consider suicide
> but I did not decide how. I struggled on and on. But
> once I realised all family members were grieving
> too, I understood my responsibility to my family, so
> I tried to maintain the routine and stability. I tried
> to discuss how each of us had coped that day.
>
> I knew I had to face and accept the agony of
> Richard never growing old. Never once did I feel
> bitter towards his friend who was the driver of the
> car; never once did I think he should have died and
> not Richard. I am thankful I more or less knew I
> should accept that Richard died in his friend's car. I
> was fortunate I could stick to that decision. I know
> I influenced Neil in particular. I know my outlook
> influenced our three other children, and I know
> my outlook eased anxiety for my parents and other
> family members.

So life continued. Neil and Flora carried out their
community responsibilities and had to rethink the
family business without Richard. It was a difficult time.

In 1971 Neil decided not to renominate for council.

He had taken over from Reg as chairman of the Arts Centre and that would keep him involved with public affairs.

In 1980 they moved into the house that Neil had built for Flora's parents on a 10-acre block years before. They built a home for her daughter Glenda and her husband John on part of the property. They planted 70 avocado trees as a new business venture and began taking annual tours of Australia. Flora was 59, Neil 60. Then life threw up another challenge.

Fifteen years later, tragedy struck a second time two days after Christmas with the sudden death of their 50-year-old son Phillip, who was in Mildura with his family on holidays and died suddenly, while playing tennis. Phillip was a teacher, an enthusiast, an energetic man who threw himself into all he did. The doctor said his heart burst, but it was later thought he had an undiagnosed heart condition. Once again Flora and Neil were devastated. For Flora this death, like Richard's 27 years earlier, 'brought a desire for relief; and an intense concern for his widow's children'. Once again they grieved, accepted, adapted and got on with their lives.

Flora and Neil moved into a retirement community in Mildura in March 2001. For nine years they lived an active and contented life together. They had a routine and Flora had a plan for each day. The highlight of the week was whichever night Glenda and John joined them for the evening meal. Flora enjoyed lectures and meeting friends at the University of the Third Age. They were intensely interested in politics and community affairs and were regular radio and television listeners, 'almost addicted to newscasts' and they both used a computer.

They have six grandchildren scattered around Australia. Flora sees them once a year. She always supplies the Christmas cakes, and chutney made with tomatoes from her Italian neighbours. They 'all share the joy of family life. I'm glad I have them; they are glad they have me.'

Neil died of a stroke on 17 October 2010. They had been together for 66 years. Flora coped with her partner's death stoically and with dignity as she had done with both her sons.

In his obituary Neil was acknowledged as one of Mildura's outstanding citizens, a man of strength and integrity who was not discouraged by controversy. Flora reminisced:

> As Neil and I aged with wonderful health I often wondered how I would behave should Neil's life end before mine. Quite strangely I cry less than I did when I was 47 and our 18-year-old died. Because I have lived in this house now for 10 years I have many acquaintances who quite freely and easily greet me with tears in their eyes and I have tears in mine. They give me a hug or a kiss. I find this really helps my morale.

At 91 Flora continues to see her life in the most positive terms. Her resilience and optimism shine through. She was in a loving partnership for most of her life and has many friends who value and draw from her lively spirit. The words Flora chooses to describe her life now are: 'free, ideal, independent, open-minded, mindful, fortunate, appreciative, aware.'

> Many envy me; most friends continue to tell me I am marvellous. I am alert enough to realise many events and circumstances contribute to my good fortune. I describe my health as as good as any 40- to 50-year-old. It's the luck of the draw. I can do everything I need to. I kneel to wash lino, I wash windows, bake cakes to excess for my families. I make fig jam, apricot jam and pick the fruit. I also make at least 40 pounds of tomato into chutney every year. Physically I do not do anything special, however my interests and obligations entail enough walking to make me wish I did not have to walk.
>
> I have not become disillusioned with age. I think I have never been disillusioned. I know lots of people who have good ideas, plans, abilities, intestinal fortitude, and commitment towards a continuing better world. Religious values have played a role to a slight degree. I chose to instil into my children—and myself, I believe—the do unto others rule. This has been my strength and support. I have not experienced any injustice or

discrimination toward me at any time even when I wasn't old.

I would be quite happy to live in care or high care when I am older. I've seen people suffering dementia and difficulties with age and it is quite clear many are better dressed and presented since going into care. Those people are relieved of decisions and responsibilities. I have never classed people as being old; I call them frail or feeble.

I have always hoped that I would not die tomorrow. I have always hoped to reach old age; I hope I get there. I think I must be old as I am older than almost everyone I know.

CHAPTER 10

THE LUCKY CAPTAIN

JOHN LOVELL 1921–

J OHN Lovell left home and family for a tough life in boarding school at age seven. He grew up resilient and adaptable, with a taste for risk and adventure. He was drawn to practical pursuits, learning technical skills, and survived a number of close calls in aircraft. His life story ranges through the Royal Naval College, bombing raids in World War Two, the loss of his wife in a tragic accident in Indonesia, a new life in running the Sydney Naval Museum, then in farming and journalism. But the Royal Navy, later the Royal Australian Navy, and flying gave John's life the most enjoyment and meaning. As an active 'oldie' he looks after himself, enjoys his extended family, participates in a local film society and travels frequently. His philosophy focuses on the future: 'Beyond the grey clouds there is lots of sunlight but you have got to plan to make use of what's ahead.'

At 92 years of age John Lovell is lucky to be alive, not because he has lived longer than most but because in so doing he has survived adventures and misadventures that would have finished off lesser men. He has been likened to a cat that has used up its full quota of nine lives.

One of the more dramatic incidents saw him come close to drowning. He was piloting a Hellcat aircraft during a training exercise, planning to land for the first time on a pint-sized escort aircraft carrier, HMS *Begum*, when his aircraft tripped over the flight deck barrier, performed a 360 degree turn and smashed into the carrier, clipping off both wings, the tail fuselage and the engine. The cockpit toppled into the depths of the Indian Ocean with John inside.

Rather characteristically, John had not prepared as he should have, failing to observe two important pre-flight instructions: he had not firmly closed the manual inflation tube on his life jacket, nor had he released his parachute harness before landing. As he sank underwater, he had time to consider his fate as the radio cord to his headset had caught in the harness release mechanism, causing John great difficulty in freeing himself. As well, the compressed air bottle, intended to inflate the life jacket and return its wearer rapidly to the surface, failed to work and the compressed air bubbled out through the open manual inflation tube. John recalls, 'According to tradition if things look really crook [as indeed they were] one is supposed to get flashbacks of important earlier life experiences. However on this occasion, I was much more interested in getting back to the surface than reviewing the past.'

By the time John managed to scramble out of the cockpit the water had become very dark indeed. He made it back to the surface with huge physical effort. Some hours later, when aboard the destroyer which had picked him up, he became seasick and up came his lunch, followed by a litre or so of salt water he had swallowed on his way back to the surface. This memory remains as vivid today as it was then.

John is an unassuming man who does not seek to impress with his exploits, though they could grace an adventure novel. He is enigmatic, but an enthusiast who loves life and enjoys company. When I first met him I was offered a convivial glass of 'rocket fuel', his family's name for a potent mix of Scotch whisky, ginger wine and water that sets you back in your chair, as I discovered. But it seems to have done John more good than harm over the years.

In a long career he served in both the British and Australian navies before he became the Executive Director of the Sydney Maritime Museum (now the

Sydney Heritage Fleet), and then a farmer, and editor of the *Milton-Ulladulla Express* on the south coast of New South Wales. He loves to travel, particularly sea cruises, and he has been passionately interested in cinema throughout his life, making his own movies and still occasionally involved with a small film society in Ulladulla. He particularly enjoys the old Busby Berkeley musicals and has his own collection. In 2012 John and his daughter Virginia visited Las Vegas, took a week's cruise on the mega-resort vessel, *Oasis of the Seas*, in the Caribbean, and an 11-week cruise from Miami through the Panama Canal along the coast of Mexico and Baja California to San Diego. John maintains a travel plan; next is a river cruise in Burma with friends.

John was born in Fort William, in the highlands of Scotland, but was there for only three weeks before being taken back to London where his father was a director of a large wholesale provisions firm. When he was two or three years old his sister Anne was born. She was 'a blue baby', an untreatable condition in those days and she died, aged one. John grew up as an only child.

He left his family and life at home at the age of seven to attend boarding school, transferring to the Royal Naval College in Dartmouth as a cadet the year he became a teenager. It was a tough life. Each boy had a sea chest for his belongings and everything had to be kept 'spick and span'. He says:

Every evening an inspection was made whilst you were lying rigid in bed and if anything was out of order you had to get up, dress in your day uniform and run around the canteen a kilometre or so away. More seriously, if you were caught fraternising with the opposite sex, drinking alcohol or smoking, you were marched up to the gym, surrounded by your peers as an armed guard, and given official 'cuts' by a PT instructor as you leaned over a vaulting horse. Strangely, on the cadet training cruises which followed the Dartmouth College era, nobody seemed to mind what you did once you were ashore.

But John was timid and slower to enjoy the company of girls and the bars in port than many of his peers.

When World War Two broke out, John, then 18, was on leave at home, standing at the window on the top floor of a batch of flats in South London. It was mid-morning on 3 September 1939; prime minister Neville Chamberlain had just made his announcement over the radio that England was at war with Germany, when suddenly the air-raid sirens started to wail. John's heart leapt as he dashed off to the bedroom for his gas mask. It was a false alarm, a British aircraft returning from Europe across the North Sea, not an enemy aircraft, had been spotted, but it foreshadowed the Blitz due to hit London and many of England's cities in less than twelve months.

The start of World War Two marked the beginning

of John's training as a midshipman, with 80 other recruits at the Royal Naval Engineering College at Keyham, alongside the naval dockyard at Devonport in the southwest county of Devon. His life as a midshipman improved significantly after the hardship of his years as a cadet.

Like many young men of the time John was impatient to be part of the war. He felt the excitement of life passing him by as he plodded along with the routine of his studies while his former peers were out there 'doing something heroic'. He loved to ride motorbikes and on one occasion, driving a mate in the sidecar of his old V Twin Enfield, he drove through a road barrier, and left his mate behind. The sidecar was never reattached.

Towards the end of 1940 the Nazis bombarded Plymouth and its surrounding districts, including the dockyard at Devonport, with firebombs. The Air Raid Precautions (ARP) sought help from the college where John was in training, and a small team of six motorcyclists was formed to carry cans of petrol to the various trailer pumps positioned around the city. John was a member of this group, initially using his old Enfield, which proved to be a poor choice as its low-slung engine collided with the debris from the bombed buildings.

The bombing usually occurred in darkness and John can vividly recall a night at the height of the Blitz when Plymouth was virtually destroyed and the whole area was lit up like Dante's Inferno. As the dangers increased and the importance of their work was recognised, the team were given new army BSA motorcycles, which they were allowed to keep. Remarkably, five out of the six survived and the leader of the team was later awarded an MBE in recognition of the motorcyclists' contribution. While the heart of Plymouth was wiped out by bombs, the nearby naval dockyard emerged largely unscathed.

As the blitzes continued, the students at the college were divided into three watches. Each night two were bussed to a developing college annex on the outskirts of Plymouth and the remaining watch stayed behind to patrol their individual quarters and stamp out any firebombs. John was billeted on the top floor of a three-storey building right alongside the dockyard. He returned one morning to find the building a heap of rubble with the duty watch irretrievably buried underneath. They had been sheltering in the basement of the building, which had been hit by chain bombs. At the age of 22, two of John's nine lives had been expended.

> We just took things as they came. I can't say we were brave, just stupid. Being stupid or, in this case, being over-enthusiastic, unfortunately led to the death of my best friend, an even keener motorcyclist. During one of the college leave periods, he volunteered to lead a column of army vehicles and, after rounding a bend, he ran smack into an oncoming truck with a fatal result.

On New Year's Eve in 1942 John and his mate Geoff—both now sub-lieutenants—joined Britain's first flat-topped aircraft carrier, HMS *Argus*. Originally an Italian passenger liner, it had been captured by the Allies in World War One and converted. During their two-year posting on board, John and Geoff acquired their Marine Engineering Watch-keeping Certificates and learned a lot about the mechanics of their ship. John also began his career in naval aviation. They made only one operational trip, escorting a convoy to Gibraltar; after that the *Argus* was relegated to deck-landing training in the River Clyde.

One highlight for John during this period was his appointment as the liaison officer to the crew for a publicity film called *The Volunteer*, which was to help in recruiting mechanics for the Fleet Air Arm. It starred Ralph Richardson, who, although lacking deck-landing experience, was able to fly the naval aircraft of the day. John would have liked to be a film director or stage producer. As a child he had set up his own cinema at home, complete with surround sound and shock coils to give his audience some extra thrills. Film remained a lifelong hobby.

Around this time the Admiralty was looking for engineers prepared to undergo flying and aircraft technical training so they could communicate with the squadron aircrew and help solve maintenance problems. As these engineers gained experience they would be posted to air stations or aircraft repair yards as test pilots. Those with particular ability could apply to attend the prestigious Empire Test Pilots' School and be used in the development and test flying of prototype naval aircraft. These naval engineers with pilot's wings were known as Flying Plumbers. Geoff opted for a future career as a submariner, whereas John was among the first to apply to join the Flying Plumbers. By the time he received his pilot's wings John had racked up 160 flying hours—85 hours solo, 15 hours night-flying and 20 hours on the link trainer.

At the beginning of 1945 he was posted to the Royal Navy's number one air-fighter school in Somerset, where he was introduced to the US-manufactured Grumman Wildcat Fighter. The power, speed and manoeuvrability of the Wildcat was far in excess of the training aircraft he had flown and at first 'a little frightening. You had to wind up the undercarriage by hand, making sure your intercom lead didn't get caught up and pull you down into the cockpit.'

While John was on leave in London, awaiting news of appointment to his first operational squadron, the war against Germany ended. He remembers being part of the crowd at Piccadilly Circus on VE night and has no idea how he got home.

But the war with Japan was not yet over and John was sent to Ceylon (now Sri Lanka). The aircraft had prolonged stopovers both at Cairo and at Karachi so

John and his compatriots had an opportunity to view the local sights. Walking down one particular street, John suddenly disappeared down an open manhole into the local sewer. He was hauled out, transferred to the RAF hospital and decontaminated. Eventually, after arriving in Colombo, he and other trainee strike pilots were transferred to the RN air station at Puttalam, whose runway had been bulldozed out of the jungle. There they progressed to flying Hellcats.

> Training included a lot of treetop-lopping low-flying and you had to roll the plane onto its back to attack the target upside down...On one of the exercises, one of my friends was flying so low that he managed to pick up a tree which got lodged in one of his wings. After all the leaves had blown off, he contacted the control tower, who ordered him to try stalling the aircraft in order to establish his stalling speed, which turned out to be considerably above normal. He was then directed to attempt a landing on the relatively short metal grid runway. He landed safely with his tyres in shreds and the trunk of the tree still stuck in the wing. So tough was that Hellcat that the dedicated maintenance crew had the aircraft flying again the very next day.

It was during his first deck landing in that Hellcat that John nearly drowned in the Indian Ocean. He was not the only one of his squadron to go over the side that day. It was a few months before the end of the war against

Japan but John never encountered the enemy in the air or on the ground. He flew about 10 missions before his squadron was sent to Singapore for the formal surrender of the Japanese to Lord Mountbatten. As far as John was aware, the only fatality his squadron suffered was an unfortunate sailor who fell down the open lift shaft of the ship while the crew was celebrating the end of the Japanese war.

John was the only one from his carrier allowed ashore to witness the official ceremony of the Japanese surrender to Lord Mountbatten at Singapore. The ceremony was held in Singapore's city hall and, following the signing of the surrender documents, the signatories and their staff emerged onto the platform outside the front entrance.

While in Singapore the ship's concert party, of which John was the spotlight operator, tried to entertain the prisoners of war being released from the Japanese prison camp at Changi. Their efforts were wasted: almost all the POWs sat there with blank expressions; John suspects that many did not realise they had been released. The war had ended before John could benefit from his training as a fighter pilot so he had mixed feelings about his lost opportunity. He remembers this time as among the happiest in his life.

In mid-December 1945, John was appointed to Maintenance Test Flying 700 Squadron, then based at Middle Wallop near Andover. For the next two years he tested aircraft and provided technical instruction to the pilots both in the air and at the ground school. As a joke, he created and used a stamp with the wording 'School of Aircraft Engineering'. It found its way into official documentation, which led to a reprimand from a higher authority who wanted to know who had created this new school.

During this period John wrote to the Air Station's Commanding Officer, who forwarded the letter to the Admiralty, stating it was high time the navy got itself involved with jet-propelled aircraft. His initiative paid off. He was sent to a course at the Gas Turbine School at Lutterworth along with a group of erudite engine designers. While he found the theory incomprehensible at first, he did well on the practical side, which involved engine testing.

Subsequently John was dispatched to the Royal Naval Air Station at Culdrose in Cornwall: there he undertook a more advanced twin-engined course on the Sea Mosquito. He had to carry out landings at night on a relatively short runway, and on one engine, a rather terrifying and dangerous experience that was later scrubbed after one trainee pilot was killed.

While stationed in the northwest of England in one of the dreariest parts of the country John met 'a cute little WREN mechanic nicknamed Smudge'. They had just begun to get to know each other when he was posted south to Yeovilton in Somerset. His adventures would continue in his new job as the Commanding Officer of 700 Naval Air Squadron.

After flying a mixture of British and American aircraft which had different brake systems—the American aircraft had foot brakes; the British aircraft used a combination of a lever on the joystick and a movement of the rudder pedals—John's foot reactions were sometimes confused. Shortly after taking over his new job he was landing a little Reliant aircraft (with foot brakes) carrying a number of local sea cadets he had taken up for a ride. He applied the brakes too harshly and the aircraft tipped over onto its back, leaving passengers and crew dangling from the roof of the cabin by their seat belts. John was severely admonished and given a new appointment, which changed the direction of his life.

The Australian government had decided that its Navy should be brought up to date by adding a fleet air arm and an aircraft carrier to its composition. John was sent to Melbourne in 1949 on loan. Meanwhile, Smudge had applied for a transfer to Yeovilton, and arrived shortly after John left. The relationship was thwarted and she and John would never see one another again, although they did correspond for a time.

> I was dispatched to Australia aboard an old Blue Funnel ship, the SS *Nestor*, which travelled around the Cape and took two months to complete its journey. Twixt Liverpool and Durban I became

enamoured with a very active 20-year-old, June, who to my chagrin advised, just before disembarking, that she was already engaged to a merchant service's officer.

But John's love life picked up as, shortly after arriving in Melbourne, he met up with 'Pooh', whose real name was Susan.

> She was the niece of A.A. Milne and, as a fluffy-haired kid, the model for Winnie the Pooh. Hence she was known by all her family and friends as Pooh. She was also the stepdaughter of an English lieutenant colonel who was on loan to the Australian Army. At the time I met her, in 1948, she was one of Melbourne's leading photographic models who appeared from time to time on the front cover of women's magazines. She worshipped her real father, who had been both an ardent Catholic and an intrepid mountaineer. As a result, encouraged by her mother, she had set her heart on becoming a nun in one of the UK's cloistered nunneries.

Despite Pooh's ambitions, and after some persistence on John's part, they became unofficially engaged but, when her stepfather was moved to Sydney and took the family with him, relations between the two became more difficult and were eventually broken off; the engagement ring was tossed down the toilet. John later heard that Pooh had joined one of the UK's most cloistered nunneries but had subsequently jumped the wall and married a stockbroker in Kent.

In the late 1940s, bachelor officers were popular among Melbourne's elite young ladies, and John found himself invited to a variety of social events. It was at one of them that he met Nancy Burgess, whose family had established a prosperous tannery in Hawthorn specialising in the production of leather for ladies' high fashion footwear. In due course the pair were married and settled in a 'shack' at Werri Beach on the New South Wales south coast, not far from the Naval Air Station at Nowra, where John was Assistant Chief Aircraft Engineer. Here, their son Christopher was born before the end of John's two-year loan period, and the family's return to the UK.

After four years in the UK, John received a letter from his father-in-law in Melbourne, inviting him to join the family business with a view to taking over its management. John retired from the Royal Navy before setting sail to Melbourne. Meanwhile, only a week before departure, Nancy gave birth to a daughter, Virginia.

After a year at the tannery, during which he put himself through a course to learn the trade, John decided this life was not for him and applied to the airlines and the navy for a job involving flying. With Nancy's encouragement he joined the RAN at his old rank of lieutenant commander and the family moved back to Nowra. He eventually became the RAN's chief aircraft engineer with the rank of acting captain. After seven years in this position, some of which was spent in Canberra away from the family, John felt ready to make way for one of the aspirants beneath him. Thus he was appointed to the position of Australian Naval Attaché in Jakarta, Indonesia: the first time that an engineer had been appointed as a Naval Attaché by the RAN.

Nancy accompanied John to Jakarta while the two children, now both in their teens, were boarded out at Melbourne grammar schools, visiting their parents in Indonesia in the school holidays. Following the Suharto coup in Indonesia, RAN vessels made a number of courtesy calls to Indonesian ports. One of the jobs of the Naval Attaché was to visit the ports ahead of each visit to make the necessary arrangements.

On one such occasion, preparing for a visit to Kupang in West Timor, normal commercial flights did not meet John's requirements. So the Indonesian navy provided their chief's personal twin-engine aircraft, complete with a crew of four as transport. Nancy was invited to join the party. As the plane took off in Kupang, John could see that it was not climbing normally and might well crash into the high ground ahead.

> I told Nancy to curl up into the crash position. Sadly, this proved to be ineffective as both she and half of the four-man crew were killed in the inevitable disaster.
>
> I came to in a nearby cottage hospital to find a

face bending over me asking if there was anything he could do. I was having trouble with breathing so asked the face, which turned out to belong to a young Australian working close by, whether he could obtain some oxygen. A short time later the face reappeared with a bottle of oxygen and some rubber tubing, located in the wreckage of the aircraft, plus a face mask, which he had fashioned out of a cocoa tin. After a few deep breaths I felt something give way in my chest and reckoned I must have had a rib stuck in my lung.

It was a long recovery and John coped with his loss through the aid of family and friends: 'I was emotionally numb.'

Among those who supported him was an old friend by the name of Laughter (La for short). John had met La in Canberra before he went to Indonesia and when he was on leave from Jakarta as Naval Attaché. After the crash she visited him in hospital and a relationship developed. 'Laughter put the joy back in my life...I don't give a lot of thought to the whys and wherefores, things just happen in life.'

La had been born in Cambridge, the daughter of an anthropologist who had spent some years in South Africa. She spent two years training as a student nurse before marrying her first husband Peter, who was a test pilot in the navy. Peter made a decision, traumatic for La at the time, that he wanted to give up his career after the war and go and live in Australia. She was very upset but agreed and the marriage, which was already under stress, limped along until 1966, when they separated.

La and John married in 1970 with La's three children and John's two children attending a quiet family event at the Naval Chapel in Watson's Bay overlooking the heads into Sydney Harbour. John's appointment after recovery was in Sydney, where La and John 'bought a small yacht and a funny little black cross Kelpie cattle dog called Robyn from the dog's home.'

When an invitation came for John to act as manager of the fledgling Sydney Maritime Museum, he accepted.

La and John sailed their 28-foot Compass yacht regularly. On a number of occasions, John took small parties of kids from deprived schools in the Sydney area on sailing excursions around the harbour. When sailing past the Naval Hospital at Balmoral with a party of primary school girls, John suggested that they might one day nurse there. 'No way,' was the reply. 'We're all going to be doctors.' They had the right idea.

John decided to leave the Sydney Maritime Museum. He and La bought Applegarth Farm in Milton, an old, somewhat primitive, stone cottage on 60 lush acres, and reinvented their lives.

> We spent a lot of energy in resurrecting the rundown farm and got together a small herd of cattle, ducks, chickens and a poddy lamb along with our black mongrel Robyn. Meanwhile our five

children—Christopher and Virginia belonging
to me, and Tim, Simon and Sue belonging to
La—were either finishing school, at university or
starting their first jobs.

John enjoyed life as a farmer but also harboured an
interest in journalism so when an opportunity arose to
become editor at the *Milton-Ulladulla Express* he changed
careers again and accepted. With a staff of two, including
a receptionist and a journalist, John spent fifteen years as
an editor and farmer. When he sold the Milton farm he
flew the whole family to Fiji for his 70th birthday. While
they sat back with gin and tonics, he walked in, loaded
down with scuba gear, ready for adventure and a new
experience.

Retirement meant John's work blended into his
hobbies. He worked on and off as a journalist until the
1990s. Over the last twenty years, while much has changed
around him, little has changed in his approach to each
day. Travel remains his great love. In 2011 he island-hopped
from Bataan in the Philippines, to Flores in Indonesia, in
a *pinisi*—the traditional Indonesian two-masted sailing
ship—and ranks the trip as the best he's ever done. 'We
are only here for a number of years—so you've got to
make the most of it.' In 2013 he travelled to Sri Lanka and
southern India with his son and daughter-in-law.

La's view of life paralleled John's. In a short memoir
she wrote: 'The most important things in life are love and
all it embraces—consideration, loyalty, honesty—then

perhaps education, everyone to their maximum ability. Lead a full rewarding life. It does not last forever and please don't call your daughter Laughter.'

La developed dementia and John reluctantly agreed with his family that she should live in the local retirement village, where she would get the necessary care. It would normally have taken a year on the waiting list but an unexpected offer of a place in the village came up. 'Both of us would have been a lot happier if she had stayed at home for another year or two,' John said. He visited La three or four times a week and felt she looked forward to his visits but communication was difficult. She passed away on 22 February 2012, after 42 years of marriage, just two days before her 88th birthday. They had been a loving, happy couple who had shared their lives together after the tragic death of John's first wife Nancy.

John says, at 91, that he is just beginning to feel the effects of old age. He misses La. He has lived a 'varied and fortunate life' and believes the ingredients of a successful long and contented life are 'a good relationship with your partner and others, good health and always having something to look forward to'. He continues to enjoy his lifelong interest in electronics and mechanical technology, even though he has trouble keeping up with new gadgets like smart phones. He is computer literate, using email, and he edits his videos and uses the internet to research his interests.

As befits the training of a naval officer, John leads a highly structured life with a regular routine.

> On a typical day I rise at 7am, make the bed, shave and shower. At 8am I have a decent breakfast and from 9.30 I shop, garden or, when La was alive, I visited her. At 12.30 I have a light lunch and from 1.30 I do my correspondence, bills or my hobbies. At 4.30pm I watch TV, a soap opera I follow—*The Bold and the Beautiful*—then I watch the news. At 5.30pm I have my pre-dinner drink, perhaps with a friend. At 7pm I have supper with TV until 10pm when I go to bed. During the winter months I am also a keen fan of the Sydney Swans.

There is no particular highlight to John's week but his family and friends are his priority along with his interests in technology, film and gardening. He has a house cleaner but does his own shopping and cooks his own meals. He has a goldfish and despite his routine and projects is sometimes lonely. But when he feels that way he will work on plans for the future, watch TV or read a book.

> As you get older it is harder to cope with the hardships of life. I worry at times about troubling news but realise it needs to be put to one side and I concentrate on something else. Everyone wants to live to an old age but they don't understand how hard it is.
>
> I have enjoyed a long life because of a good

upbringing (thanks to my parents) and lots of luck. And rocket fuel. Beyond the grey clouds there is lots of sunlight but you have got to plan to make use of what's ahead.

CHAPTER 11

THE SCIENTIST WHO BECAME AN ARTIST

MURIEL CRABTREE 1908–2010

MURIEL Crabtree was a great achiever in an age of blue-stocking feminism. She was a biochemist, published academic, teacher and vice-principal at Melbourne University College, the first college for women at an Australian university. She triumphed as a scholar and mentor and was a brave and curious voyager who travelled the Old Silk Road and went to remote places where few women ventured alone. On retirement from University College she had a teaching career at the University of the Third Age, then reinvented herself as an artist. Her pastels, drawn over two decades, were shown at an exhibition opened by the

Governor-General at University College six weeks after she died. A caring but tough-minded individual, she lived independently until a fall resulted in her being placed in a care facility where she fought against its dehumanising regimen. Her story is a classic case highlighting why mindful purpose in life is paramount until we die.

At the age of 102, Muriel was living independently in her own unit within a retirement village at Donvale. She had lived there 20 years. She liked to swim most days in the heated community pool, which helped maintain muscle strength in her legs. She cooked for herself. Each week she would make a large stew with meat and lots of vegetables, which she divided for eating throughout the week. All the possessions that mattered to her, which she had gathered throughout her long life, were placed around the rooms, along with her many books. Her paintings covered the walls.

As a former academic and teacher she enjoyed working and helped catalogue the 6000 books in the village library. She had also focused on developing her drawing skills over more than 20 years, becoming very competent with pastels, and there was a room in the facility where she set up her easel and drew her pastel portraits and landscapes. Her art work was more than a hobby; it had become her career. She attended the Victorian Artists' Society twice a week to draw the live models provided and to have social contact with those who had a common interest. She had a regular taxi driver to transport her and he became a supportive friend who would help her up the steps at the entrance. Muriel was admired for the way she looked after herself, and she was content with the life she had created at her advanced age.

At 102, Muriel had become frail. One night she fell in her unit; an ambulance was called and she was sent to hospital. Once there she learned that she would not be allowed to return to her home; the governing committee had ruled that, as there was no nurse on duty at night to care for someone who might need help, Muriel must move where such care would be provided and her unit would be sold under the agreement made when she entered the village.

So Muriel lost her independence. She never married and has no children. Many of her friends had died. Her only relatives were her deceased brother's only son and his wife, who lived in Sydney. They took on the responsibility of finding a place for Muriel to live. They looked around Melbourne for a suitable care residence as Muriel wanted to stay where she had lived for most of her life and they finally settled on a facility in Melbourne's eastern suburbs that seemed ideal.

But Muriel hated her new home. She felt she had been incarcerated. She was angry that she had lost her independence. The most upsetting thing for her was that there was no place for her to do her pastel drawings. She was told she could not draw in her room, that pastel dust got on the floor and staff had to keep cleaning it up. Muriel made suggestions to resolve the situation. She asked if she could set up her easel in the bathroom, but management said it was against regulations. There was no craft room for the residents and no available space anywhere in the building. Her niece-in-law told Muriel she had to conform. She stressed that Muriel must accept this accommodation and 'behave herself' as there was nowhere else for her to go but a nursing home. The one thing that gave Muriel's life interest and meaning was being taken from her. As a result, not surprisingly, she felt angry, worn down and depressed.

Before her fall Muriel's main pleasure in life was her pastel drawing. She had toyed with the idea of an exhibition as she had about 50 pictures to her credit but now her work and plans had to come to an end. You need space to draw. You need to be able to move backwards and forwards around an easel, especially if you are working with a model, and Muriel did not see why this should not still be possible. 'I will leave money to replace the carpet in my will. This is my room; I should be able to draw in my room, at least. This place is a jail; only in jail you might get more services—classes, art books.'

But the facility had no expectation that any of its 'inmates' would be involved in creative work. The flexible service they said they offered did not include finding a way to cater for the one activity that would occupy, motivate and provide some joy for a woman with a talent and her wits about her to engage in for her remaining life.

Muriel wanted to have her drawings around her room. She placed them against the walls where she wanted them to be hung. She had been in her new room for some weeks when I first came to visit and half the pictures were still propped up where she had first placed them. 'A workman had appeared,' she told me, 'but he said he was not allowed to put a picture hook in a solid brick wall as it would cause damage. He worked for about half an hour and just went off.' He didn't say anything to Muriel about where he was going. When you are 102 and sitting in the corner of the room day after day you don't carry a lot of authority, so the workman had not bothered explaining what he intended to do. And he did not return.

This fuelled Muriel's anger: 'It's my room. I am paying for it, but no, they say, the inspector will come and it's a bad mark for them. They don't like me spilling things on the floor. They don't like me to be untidy, oh no, they don't like that.'

Muriel needed something to place her rubbish in; no wastepaper basket was provided. She needed a container for her glasses and the TV remote; two essentials for her limited lifestyle. Her niece-in-law resolved these issues by getting her a bin and a plastic box for the important things Muriel could not afford to mislay.

So there Muriel sat each day, in an armchair facing

three walls, with her back to the only window in the room, her bed to her right, a television at the end of the bed. There was one extra chair for a visitor to occupy and a spacious bathroom which enabled a carer to help Muriel shower and dress. Some pictures were hung but the wall she faced directly was bare. Her pictures would remain propped on the floor until she left the room for the last time.

Muriel was weakened by osteoarthritis; her knees hurt her all the time. She walked with a frame and was quite unstable but her general health was good for her years. Her skin got itchy but staff rubbed in a cream and massaged her, which relieved it. She was prepared for bed and helped to get in and out. She saw the physio once a week as well as the hairdresser. Muriel was assisted getting to meals but soon decided she did not want to go to the dining room, not because she could not manage her walking frame but because each time she was seated at the same table with a couple who did not speak a word. The man never addressed his wife in public and did not address the other inmates. Given the company available, Muriel preferred to spend her time knitting, reading the newspaper, and watching television in her room.

Muriel was devastated by what had happened to her and the situation she found herself in. She maintained her fiery spirit when she discussed her predicament but she had no family member to plead her case. Her niece-in-law in Sydney had no intention of going in to bat for her aunt's right to draw in her room, and Muriel believed she could not ask for anything. She had one front tooth missing and was embarrassed by her appearance. 'I try to keep my mouth closed when I talk,' she said. The preparatory dental work had been done and the dentist was ready to fix her tooth whenever Muriel was able to get to see him, but there were too many obstacles in the way. 'They tell me I have no money,' Muriel said and she had nothing in her purse. So a trip to the dentist and the help needed to get into and out of a taxi were more than Muriel could deal with. Unquestionably, her physical needs were met in the care accommodation but Muriel's emotional, intellectual and social needs were not, and her self-esteem suffered.

She expressed her frustration:

> With nobody to talk to I am talking inwardly now; trying to work out some way of living. I don't know how to cope. I am at an absolute loss. It's a horrible feeling. I would like to have avoided this and I think as a rule a long life is a bad thing. I don't think it's good to live too long unless you have lots of relations and friends, but still you are imposing on them. And I think it is very difficult when you are old to fit into what's going on and if I could I wouldn't mind dying tonight.
>
> There is nothing more I can do; the painting was something. I wanted to see how far I could go with that. They do seem to be wiping it out for me and I don't know what to do next, to do now. Nothing!

On the whole I think it would be much better if you lived to about 60 and then called it a day. I think you can cope until 60. You can keep intact. You can keep your own personality. You are not being imposed on. You are not being forced to do anything. You can do what you want.

What I had has been taken from me. I have nothing now and so I don't see any point to my living any longer, but if I had relations or young people growing up that would be different. I would like to see that but I haven't any personal thing to belong to so I think it's just a waste. I would like to find some way in which I could be useful or do something that would be of value to somebody. But not this; just hovering, just existing, I can't cope with this. No.

I felt angry that this remarkable, intelligent woman, a pioneer in so many ways who had contributed so much in her lifetime should be placed in this invidious situation by a system that simply took care of the physical needs of inmates and neglected their essential social and intellectual needs. This was a tragic dilemma for Muriel Crabtree and not the way to end any life.

The first time I came to visit Muriel in care I felt ambivalent about her new home. The door was locked with an electronic code and I had to wait to be admitted by a woman who escorted me to Muriel's room. Muriel was seated, as was usual, in her armchair. Her face lit up when she saw me and she started talking immediately about her telephone and the problems she had been having connecting with people. In her isolated situation, desperate for conversation and company, the phone was her lifeline. She still had a small group of people who remained in contact so she was quite upset that she could not master the phone. She was finding she either didn't hear the phone or she would miss a call if she left the room, so she did not want to go anywhere.

Muriel, who was a little deaf, clearly needed help in understanding the telephone; she was smart, she just needed some time spent training and a list of written instructions. But no one had taken the time to teach her the fundamentals. Muriel thought her friend Lesley Falloon had someone answering her phone as there was always somebody talking when she called. 'I try to get in first and speak quickly but I don't get a response.' I explained Lesley had an answering machine; it was a recorded voice but Lesley would get her message. She was unsure how to check her own messages so I explained she needed to call 101.

When we went to sit in the dining room for afternoon tea it did not take long to understand Muriel's dilemma. The facility, although physically clean and comfortable, was depressing. Most of the inmates looked like tragic figures: grey and hunched over their walking frames. They sat in isolation with blank faces. I did not see two people sitting together in conversation when I was there. There was a seating area beyond the dining room with a large television set turned on. Muriel said she went there at first to try to find somebody to talk to but she didn't go there anymore.

> They are all so boring. I can't think of anything to say to them and they have nothing to say. They walk around with their frames all bent up, looking terrible. Why haven't their doctors taught them to stand up straight—it can't be good for their internal organs. I prefer isolation and eating alone in my room to sharing the company on offer, but the staff insist I can't be antisocial.

Looking around the room, I had to agree silently with Muriel's position on this. Most in the facility were dementia patients and they were not going to provide the mental stimulation Muriel craved. She had to fend off someone coming into her room to take her favourite painting, one left propped by the wall. It made her anxious so she asked that Lesley take it and keep it safe. Muriel asked me if I knew of anyone interesting who might come and talk to her, as she craved conversation.

As I was leaving there was a wide-eyed woman walking the corridors who came up to me at the door. She asked me if I had a pain in my stomach. I said I didn't. She thought I did because I had my arm across my front. She then began to take off her blouse and I asked what she was doing. She said she wanted to give it to me. I replied that I didn't want it so she pulled it back down.

She stood trying to open the front door. I punched in the code, said, 'Excuse me, I'm sorry but you have to stay here.' She repeated, 'I have to stay here.' The visit had upset me. This was no way for Muriel to end her days.

Muriel was born on 9 April 1908. She was a remarkable woman. She had lived a long and active life. She was a biochemist, a teacher and artist; she was widely travelled and courageously independent, accomplishing things most women of her era would never have attempted. She was a quiet achiever, never one to claim the centre of attention, but a role model for hundreds of students who, like me, attended Melbourne University Women's College during her years there as Vice-Principal.

UWC was a pioneering institution, which was established in 1937 with seven students after a long and difficult political struggle. It took 16 years to get recognition of the need for such a college, to find a suitable site and secure the funds with which to build. It aimed to provide an education equal in status to the four men's colleges at Melbourne University at the time—Ormond, Trinity, Newman and Queen's. Muriel, philosophically a strong feminist but not one to make a fuss about it, had a close involvement with UWC for almost 50 years.

She was born in Launceston, Tasmania, and spent her early years attending Launceston Church Girls Grammar School, where she was regarded as 'a clever girl'. She had a smart older brother and she was once accused of having him do her homework: a girl couldn't be that smart. But indeed she was. Her parents were not trained professionals. Her father was a land speculator and had obviously done well, and he and her mother were enlightened in encouraging both children to pursue higher study. The family moved to Melbourne in 1925 for Muriel's tertiary education. At a time when few girls went to university and fewer studied science she gained her Bachelor of Science in 1930 and her Master of Science in Biochemistry with first-class honours in March 1931. The same year she was awarded a government grant to continue her research in the Department of Biochemistry at Melbourne University. Some of her work was published in the *Journal of Physiology* that year.

In August 1932, in another ground-breaking achievement, she was awarded a graduate scholarship to attend Bryn Mawr College in Philadelphia, one of the five most notable women's colleges in the US. Following an academic year at Bryn Mawr, Muriel travelled to England where she stayed for four and a half years. For three of those years she held research grants from the British Medical Research Council carrying out investigations into iodine metabolism. Some of this work was published in the Medical Research Council's special report in 1936.

During this time Muriel spent several weeks in the laboratories of the Department of Health at Bern, Switzerland, studying a micro-method for the estimation of iodine, under the direction of Professor von Fellenberg. Muriel continued with this line of research when she came back to Australia in February 1938 to take up a position as research biochemist in the Department of Medicine at the University of Sydney for two years, working under the direction of Professor Victor Trikojus. Muriel claimed she never experienced discrimination. Although the men got the lectureships and the women were the demonstrators it did not bother her. She went from one achievement to another anyway.

At the age of 31 her remarkable career was interrupted by the war. She took up teaching and in July 1940 became a science mistress at the New England Girls' School in Armidale. At the end of 1941 she returned to her discipline as senior demonstrator in the Department of Biochemistry at Melbourne University where she was later promoted to lecturer, retaining the role until 1966.

Muriel entered UWC in 1943 as a graduate resident when Dr Hort was principal. A little later she was appointed resident tutor in Biochemistry. She became acting principal when Dr Hort went to Europe on leave and remained in that role until Myra Roper's appointment as principal. Myra was another exceptional woman who had studied at Cambridge. She was assertive and outspoken and soon developed a media profile in Melbourne. She strongly encouraged each girl who entered UWC to take responsibility for their lives, to be active, outspoken and to be confident in their own worth.

Myra and Muriel were a great partnership. Myra looked after the politics and the fundraising and Muriel ran the college for a period of 17 years. Both women had opted not to marry. It was a decision that in later years Muriel regretted. In retrospect she thought it 'a foolish decision. I made a mistake. I was expecting too much of a partner.' Myra, too, was ambivalent, lamenting that single women were not in high demand as dinner party invitees but adding, in reflecting on her life, 'Being an old maid isn't a bad thing. Being on the shelf can be very interesting. You can get a view of life and what is going on.'

Both Myra and Muriel lived very independent lives and diffused their maternal instincts by caring for the young women in UWC. Their early years in office were for building and development, an exciting time for the college, which expanded its student numbers from 43 to 131 with the building of two new wings, a new dining hall and kitchen.

'Crab', as Muriel was affectionately called by the students, was well liked for her gentleness and kind ways. She was devoted to and protective of the girls. The celebrated duo, nicknamed the M&Ms, made a rather formidable pair: one remembered fondly for her authority and status as a role model for the students, the other no less a role model for the kindness and affection she showered upon the girls. Muriel is also widely remembered for her interest in and knowledge of art, for the interesting paintings and prints on her walls, her sculptures and other *objets d'art*, all of which helped broaden the knowledge of students. UWC became 'the place to be' for female students and there was particular encouragement given to country and Asian students. I was a beneficiary of their influence over four years as a student in college in the 1950s. I look back on those years as among the most formative and enjoyable of my life.

After Myra's retirement Muriel continued as vice-principal for some months before returning to full-time work in the Biochemistry School in 1961. The friendship remained firm and they bought a house together. Muriel lived a full life. She travelled with Myra to many countries, including China, at a time when few Westerners were given entry. These two women were held in high regard by the Chinese government and they always tried to find educational opportunities in Australia for the young female students they met.

Muriel travelled the Old Silk Road, and to Thailand, Cambodia, India, Nepal, Indonesia, Ethiopia, Kenya, Uganda, Mexico and Papua New Guinea, often visiting students who had been resident in college. She showed great courage going to remote places where few women ventured alone, taking small boats and planes into the unknown. On her retirement in 1968 Muriel remained active for a further eight years as a teacher at the University of the Third Age (U3A) giving talks on China and the Silk Road. She had taken hundreds of slides over the years, which she used to illustrate her talks; she developed a wide following.

Muriel had a great capacity to reinvent herself and now that she had the time she could focus on painting and pastel drawing, which had always been a major interest; this became the centre of her life. But, in her final years, her desire to keep drawing was bringing her into conflict with her carers.

I returned home after my visit to Muriel and told my husband Don—like Muriel he had taken up painting in semi-retirement—of her situation. We decided to act quickly. I phoned Lesley Falloon, who had been visiting and supporting Muriel throughout her retirement. I suggested we arrange an exhibition of Muriel's pastels and get her drawing again. Lesley suggested we call ourselves the Committee, which Muriel would relate to and which would give the idea status.

Don bought drawing paper and a new box of pastels and took them out to Muriel. We encouraged her to draw, regardless of the rules. Muriel felt she needed a model or images that would motivate ideas. Don downloaded some pictures and Muriel began to look through newspapers and magazines. We informed her that she had a committee of three who were going to organise her art exhibition. We insisted she must begin her pastel drawings again as we wanted to make sure there were current works in the exhibition that would show what an active 102-year-old was capable of producing.

The three of us visited Muriel together to discuss the exhibition and to work out the logistics. We succeeded in our purpose: Muriel was motivated to try to draw even in her restricted living conditions and the claim that she had a committee working on her exhibition was enough to give the facility's administration pause about the prohibition they had placed on her drawing. Muriel was a modest woman but the idea of a committee planning an exhibition of her work obviously pleased her. She began to perk up.

Muriel began to draw. At first Don organised a simple clipboard to which she could attach her working paper, but quite independently a visitor passing by her door, there to see someone else, realised Muriel needed an easel and got one for her. I phoned the new principal of University College, Dr Jennifer McDonald, to see if she would be willing to hold an exhibition at the college. She was enthusiastic and saw it as an event that past students would be interested in attending. The committee wanted someone of standing to open the exhibition and I decided the Governor-General, Quentin Bryce, was just the person we needed to give the event the profile it deserved.

The Governor-General had been a member of my board for nine years when I was Director of the Australian Children's Television Foundation. I thought the idea of an exhibition for Muriel would appeal to her; it was a good fit with her interests. Quentin is a strong advocate for women and in an earlier life was Chair of the National Women's Advisory Council. She had also been the principal and CEO of the Women's College at the University of Sydney for five years. I emailed the Governor-General's appointments secretary describing the event and asking if she would be available to open the exhibition.

Don and I went to the storage building where Muriel's pictures had been moved when she left her unit in the village. There were in excess of 60 framed and unframed portraits and landscapes. It was an impressive body of work so we decided to take them all to college. Muriel, who was now quite excited about the upcoming exhibition, was telling her relatives, friends and the staff looking after her that she had a committee that was organising her exhibition. Her status in the care accommodation improved immediately. I received a call from her niece-in-law, who was rather stroppy as Muriel had told her that if she wanted to know about the exhibition she could speak to her committee. The niece insisted Muriel 'was destroying the carpet'. I was curt. It was clearly an exaggeration and of less importance in the scheme of things than Muriel's well-being. I was pleased to hear that she was indeed drawing.

Muriel collapsed on the morning of 13 December 2010. She was taken by ambulance to Box Hill Hospital, where they diagnosed a severe stroke with paralysis down one side. I rang the hospital to ask whether I could visit. They encouraged me to come so Don and I went to see her. She was propped up in bed, looking very frail. A speech therapist came to swab Muriel's mouth and Muriel seemed to welcome the assistance. The therapist explained she would be kept comfortable and that following Muriel's wishes, which were to have no intervention, they would not attempt to feed her other than keep her on a drip.

When people are near death there is a lot of speculation by concerned friends about what the patient can hear and what they can't hear. I have no idea if Muriel knew we were there. She did not speak but her eyes were open and she looked at us and made some sounds of acknowledgment. I told her about our progress with the exhibition, but couldn't yet say Quentin had accepted. I was waiting to hear from her administrative assistant. I received that advice on 16 December: the Governor-General would be pleased to open the exhibition. Muriel died on 18 December without knowing that her exhibition would go ahead with the Governor-General officiating. We had come close to fulfilling her plan but not quite close enough.

For all her achievements and her fortitude, Muriel was a most unassuming person; she did not like a fuss to be made over her. But it would have brought her great pleasure to be present at a function which celebrated her life achievements and was a culmination of her artworks drawn from the last 20 years of her long life. Muriel had left her body to the university and so there would be no funeral. There was to be no memorial; nothing was planned by the relatives. It was difficult not to get the impression that Muriel was an old woman who had become too much trouble to deal with.

The committee met with the college principal and decided to proceed with a celebration of Muriel's life, artistry and leadership on 15 February 2011. The Governor-General looked resplendent, as always, in a bright green suit and matching spike heels with a purple bunch of violets (signifying women) on her lapel. She made a great speech and Muriel's niece-in-law and nephew and all her extended family were there to pay tribute to their aunt. They were first in line to meet the Governor-General.

Quentin spoke of Muriel as a leader, as one of the women 'who sat in the lecture halls and earned their academic merit and eminence alongside men ... a woman who applied her immense intelligence, courage, vision and creativity to securing women's right and freedom to learn and enter the professions.'

She paid tribute to Muriel's early pioneering life as a scientist, teacher, scholar, mentor, and brave and curious voyager.

University College established an award in Muriel Crabtree's name for Women in Leadership, and her pastel drawings, those that were not purchased by past students who attended the exhibition, were framed to hang on the walls of the residential University College. She would have been thrilled.

CHAPTER 12

MR MILDURA

REGINALD ETHERINGTON

1905–2000

MY parents had positive attributes in abundance, and I understand now that this is why I didn't notice they were ageing. Reg was an initiator, always in charge, and Eva was the ideal partner for a man like that. She was content running a household and raising a family. Their origins were working class. They knew how to work hard and their core values stemmed from family and community life. They created a very happy home to grow up in.

For more than three-quarters of a century Reg Etherington was actively engaged in Mildura and in northern Victoria, as a businessman, city councillor and as chair of a host of other cultural, local government and community initiatives. He was known either as Mr

Mildura, or Mr Fix-it or, by those who crossed him, as Mr Right. Reg Etherington was personable, energetic, strategically patient and far-sighted. He was loved by many and opposed bitterly by others. He was also my father, a great dad who influenced me in many ways and lived his long life as though he would never fade away. My mother was his support and could rise to the occasion when public life demanded. Purpose drove them and they had the ability to reinvent it as their lives evolved.

Reg planned and guided much of Mildura's development: not just its roads, water, sewerage, electricity and sporting amenities, but also its cultural facilities. The arts were seen as non-essential by the community at large. Why spend money on a gallery when you could build more roads, footpaths and sporting ovals? Reg was exceptional in arguing for a cause, overcoming objections and solving financial issues. He would say, 'If an idea is good enough the funds will fall out of the sky.' And somehow they did. He felt Mildura already had more than enough roads, bridges and sporting facilities. He argued the community needed to preserve and value its own heritage. He went on to initiate the Regional Art Galleries Association for country galleries across Victoria.

Reg was born in Faversham, Kent, on 28 January 1905. His father was a tradesman, a carpenter and joiner. Such skills were needed in Australia and Reg's parents decided to migrate in 1912; it was a courageous decision to travel with a large brood to a new land. Reg was seven years old, the fourth child and third boy in a family of six children; another boy would be born in Australia. For a seven-year-old the sea voyage was an adventure made somewhat disturbing by the news of *Titanic* sinking not long before they sailed. That disaster stayed on Reg's mind through the long journey. The family settled in Thornbury, a northern suburb of Melbourne, where Reg attended Wales Street State Primary School and then University High School on a scholarship. 'We were very close-knit as a family. I was the one who left home. We got on well together, had a happy life, enough to eat and drink, and we went to Sunday School.'

When Reg left school he decided to become apprenticed as a watchmaker and jeweller. He was working in Balaclava for a Mr Lawrence, who did work for Horace Hammerton, a jeweller in Mildura. Hammerton was looking for an apprentice willing to come to Mildura for £10 a week and a promise of a future share in the profits. Reg heard about the opportunity, applied and got the job. He arrived in Mildura on 1 December 1924 aged 19, excited and ready for anything. At that time Mildura was a salinated dust bowl, a small irrigation settlement on the Murray River with few facilities, but Reg was open to the challenge of forging a future there. He made friends through the Methodist Church, where he sang in the choir. He went fishing and shooting, grew familiar with the Mallee bush and the Murray River environs and settled into life in the remote community. He applied himself to his work, studying optometry by correspondence part-time and obtaining the degree of Fellow of the Victorian Optical Association. He was number 21 on the register and became the first qualified resident optometrist in Mildura.

Four years after his arrival, and after surviving typhoid fever, Reg decided to settle in Mildura. He had his eye on a young woman, Eva Ellis, who also sang in the church choir. Eva worked at White's Shoe Store. He courted her and they decided to marry. Reg wanted security for the future he planned with Eva so he asked Mr Hammerton for a formal agreement acknowledging the promised profit share. But Hammerton wasn't prepared to give him a written agreement. 'Don't be silly, Reg,' he said. 'Trust me.' So Reg gave a week's notice and decided to set up in business against his employer. 'I'll see you go broke,' was Hammerton's response. Reg went to see his older brother Arthur, an accountant in Melbourne, who spoke to Hammerton and was told that he would run Reg out of Mildura. 'We'll see about that,' said Arthur, who assisted his 24-year-old brother in getting a bank loan.

It was an audacious move but typical of young Reg, who was by nature a risk-taker. Anger is a great motivator and Reg was outraged by what he considered a betrayal of trust by Hammerton: he was determined to succeed. He did not lack confidence and he was prepared to work hard. While the old established Mildura families watched and waited for Reg to go broke, he prospered. He developed his optometry business and worked long hours to be a success. He had a way with people and they liked him: he was gregarious; he had a great laugh and loved a good yarn. Although the 1930s were tough years to be starting a business, Reg gained a loyal following. His working-class roots gave him an understanding and easy connection with men who laboured with their hands, the blockies who were growing citrus and vines in the pioneering agricultural settlement of Mildura. But the women also liked him. He would joke, he was kind and generous to his clients, allowing them to pay when they could afford it.

The town was undeveloped, with no paved roads, footpaths, sewerage system or sporting facilities, when Reg married Eva on 7 October 1931. Eva Ellis was born in Albury on 1 February 1908. Her family lived in the small town of Bethanga twenty miles away. For many years Eva walked a mile to school after she had milked half-a-dozen cows. Her mother Evelyn's family owned a property and had been long established in Australia but Evelyn married a man who would not settle to any occupation in life and drifted from one job to another, dissipating his wife's inheritance as he went. For William Ellis, the pastures were always greener somewhere else. From Bethanga the family moved to a dairy farm at Nar Nar Goon, then to a sheep property in Violet Town, then a wheat farm in Perponda and another at Carwarp, before they came eventually to Mildura. Each move proved costly so they lived modestly in Mildura in a small house near the railway track.

Eva stayed home and helped her mother, while her two brothers went to school. Her first paid job was at Washington's department store in the music section, before she moved to White's, where she was working when she first met Reg. When they married they moved into 13 Sarnia Avenue, where they would live for the next 67 years. Reg paid £500 for the house, putting down a deposit of £50. The Commonwealth Bank lent them the money, to be paid off over 26 years. They had £10 left in their kitty to begin family life and Eva's housekeeping budget was £2 a week. She was a frugal housekeeper and throughout her married life kept a notebook detailing her household expenses. Even in more affluent times she did not change the habit.

Eva loved flowers and Reg created a garden for her. They entered a gardening competition soon after moving into their new home. On the day of the judging he dug up the flowers from the backyard and replanted them in the front garden to make a good display. He won the competition and was very proud of his silver cup. Reg planted a small Norfolk pine in the front garden, which grew to a great height over the years, well beyond the roof line, lifting the pavement at the side of the house until it was difficult to walk along the footpath. But he refused to trim it and the tree continued growing, showering the roof and filling the gutters with pine needles until after his death in 2000, when the house was sold. It became the tallest tree in the city of Mildura, a landmark on the flat terrain; arriving by air or road we always knew where our house was.

In 1932 Reg bought into Wilson's jewellery business in a historic art deco building on Deakin Avenue, the main street of town. In his first move to take care of his siblings, he brought his older brother Jim from Melbourne to run the jewellery business, which remains under the Etherington name today. Between 1933 and 1937 Reg and Eva had three daughters; I was the youngest. While Eva was caring for the family Reg was working long hours, and his punishing routine led to a breakdown in health. The doctor advised him to go to Queensland to recuperate, and to find a hobby that could relax him. So in the late 1930s Reg bought a fruit block in Karadoc Avenue, Irymple, three miles out of town where he could go each weekend and do physical labour. This became part of a lifelong routine which no doubt helped keep him fit and provided him with thinking time for his many plans and projects. He built up an orange orchard and poultry farm and later he raised cattle. He brought his younger brother Alec from Melbourne to run the block and his youngest brother, Les, also came to Mildura to work in the optometry business. He looked after his extended family.

Like all men of his generation, he had desperately wanted a son to carry on the family name, a boy he could take shooting and fishing, who could continue the family business. As the third daughter and final try, I was a disappointment, but Reg reconciled admirably to his lack of a male heir. He was a very good father who loved his girls. He was strict yet caring. His word was final; he was not a man to be challenged. I remember only one beating with his razor strop but it was deserved. Family was very important to him. We did not go to bed at night without a story, usually one he made up about a fantasy character called Topsie Trix, and although he seemed to be out every night of the week he was there at mealtimes and to put us to bed. He taught us to swim and ride horses and encouraged us to play musical instruments. When the circus was in town he would take us, and we went regularly to the seaside at Glenelg in South Australia for holidays. He promised us each a watch when we learned to swim. As the third child I learned earlier than my sisters and he offered me the choice of a watch or a twin choc ice-cream. He figured delayed gratification was not my strong suit at age six and he was right; I chose the twin choc. He would take us for walks and drop money down the leg of his trousers. We would scurry along behind Mum and Dad gathering coins and the occasional note, and at the end of the walk we could buy an ice-cream. He was good fun.

At Sarnia Avenue we lived in one room, the dining

room next to the kitchen. The lounge room was used only when visitors came. The dining room had a fire in winter and was the only warm area in the house other than the kitchen. After tea in the evening the family gathered around the radio. Dad had a comfortable armchair, Mum an upright chair where she could knit, and we girls sat around the table on the rather uncomfortable dining chairs Dad had made. (He made all the furniture in the house, having learned carpentry from his father.) In the evening we played cards, board games, listened to the radio and did our homework. Reg had the phone beside his chair and it seemed he was always on it.

I grew up in a household where politics were as familiar to me as the values of the Methodist Church where I went to Sunday School. It seemed nothing of any importance happened in Mildura that my father was not involved in, and I never sensed any dirty business. My father was straight and direct: he always had a clear vision of what he was trying to achieve and he gained support for his ventures by the sheer force of argument. I heard much of what went on over the phone without even knowing I was listening. I observed as men came to the house with their problems to seek my dad's advice. Mildura was a community where everyone knew everyone, and when I was growing up, everyone knew Reg Etherington.

My father retired from optometry in 1952, when he

was 47. His brother Les took over the business. Reg had invested in commercial properties, financing each one with an insurance policy and covering the borrowings with rental income, and by 1952 he felt the family had enough income to live on: making money was not his priority. He stood for council, wanting to devote his time to public service, and for more than 40 years that is what he did. Eva did the same. Apart from her work as a housewife, which she did exceptionally well (she was a great cook and washed and ironed clothes as if they came out of a professional laundry), her interests were the Red Cross, the Country Women's Association, the Deaf Auxiliary, and the church. She paid for and arranged the flowers in the Methodist Church every Saturday for 20 years from 1946.

I now realise my parents were unusual in their commitment to the community, but when I was growing up in Mildura I took our life for granted, absorbing the values and the work ethic and expecting that the place to be in life was at the centre of the action. The tasks Reg took on weren't easy; I learned that change is not a simple process. His causes often made him enemies but the satisfaction he gained was in the tangible benefit he saw resulting from his political efforts.

He found wisdom in reading classics and he particularly enjoyed Shakespeare and Charles Dickens. He would mark in pencil the pages that caught his eye, and he would often craft speeches around the ideas he took from literature. A passage in *Little Dorrit* was particularly pertinent, summing up his feelings about the people he met in public life and the effort involved in implementing change:

> It is true that How not to do it was the great study and object of all public departments and professional politicians all round the Circumlocution Office. It is true that every new premier and every new government, coming in because they had upheld a certain thing as necessary to be done, were no sooner come in than they applied their utmost faculties to discovering How not to do it. It is true that from the moment when a general election was over, every returned man who had been raving on hustings because it hadn't been done, and who had been asking the friends of the honourable gentleman in the opposite interest on pain of impeachment to tell him why it hadn't been done, and who had been asserting that it must be done, and who had been pledging himself that it should be done, began to devise, How it was not to be done. It is true that the debates of both Houses of Parliament, the whole session through, uniformly tended to the protracted deliberation, How not to do it.

In contrast Reg was a study in how to get things done. In October 1999 *The Sunraysia Daily* published a profile on Reg entitled 'Etherington vision was a treasure to behold'. Reg was proud of his achievements and once said to me: 'I'm an initiator, that's my nature. So much was needed in Mildura. There is little in this town that was worthwhile that I wasn't involved in.'

And reminiscent of *Little Dorrit* he spoke about his experience of people:

> Public life is an interesting thing. People get in there supposedly for the community, but when they get there, they enjoy the personal kudos; they forget the rest of it and become despots. They're not interested in the next generation; they're only interested in the next balance sheet... All most of them have ever done is complain about what's wrong with something that's already there.

Reg was a cultured man, well educated, well read, with a keen interest in literature and ideas. He was, above all, a thinker. As his tribute outlines, one of his greatest achievements was his legacy to the arts. The other was his pioneering work manufacturing the world's first wide-angle lenses for rocket research.

When R.D. Elliott, the proprietor of *The Sunraysia Daily*, offered his art collection to the city of Mildura in 1944, there was the problem of where and how to house it. Rio Vista, the mansion built by the Chaffey brothers, Mildura irrigation pioneers, was up for sale. Reg, with the assistance of the town clerk, Bill Downie, devised a scheme that overcame the objections of those on council who did not want ratepayers' money spent on the arts. They sold the town's large generating plant to the State Electricity Commission, thus gaining funds to buy Rio Vista, garner the Elliott collection for the city and provide relief from ongoing power generating costs.

It was a brilliant piece of financial management whereby the council paid only £18,000 for Rio Vista and nothing for the construction of the art gallery. Later on Reg threw his weight behind the development of an arts centre, gallery and performing arts theatre, as chairman of the Building Committee for 14 years. Although he won the argument, his opponents were unrelenting, waging a campaign claiming Reg was wasting ratepayers' money on the arts. Ultimately Reg would be kicked off the council at an election over this issue but he still ensured the job was done. The new Mildura Arts Centre opened in 1966.

The 1950s have been called the Cactus Years in terms of the arts in Australia, but they proved to be astonishingly rich. The cultural cringe was challenged by Australian artists, the Menzies government built on postwar prosperity and new premier Henry Bolte asserted Victoria's right to a place in the sun, pushing large civil works, encouraging new business and, ironically for such a conservative man, giving much public support to the arts. The 1953 *Herald* Outdoor Art Show gave the public a taste for modern art and in 1956 Eric Westbrook's appointment as Director of the National Gallery of Victoria extended that movement.

Bolte passed legislation to make a start on building the new arts centre in St Kilda Road, and Reg was appointed to the Melbourne Arts Centre Building Committee to represent regional Victoria. He did not accept that cultural endeavours should be centred solely in major cities and wanted a share of the new arts funding for regional areas including Mildura, so he met with leading figures to discuss forming a new group to promote regional galleries.

As part of this initiative, the established regional galleries of Bendigo, Ballarat, Castlemaine and Geelong wanted their share of state funding. The group first met at the National Gallery of Victoria and Reg, with Geelong art teacher Don Webb and supported by Eric Westbrook, successfully lobbied for funds from the state government to support regional galleries in Mildura, Hamilton, Shepparton, Swan Hill and Benalla.

When Hamilton was offered the Sandby watercolour collection, local chemist Ted Dempster, the mayor at the time, was vilified for supposedly running the city into debt. Reg urged him to hold firm and it was Dempster's casting vote as mayor that secured the future of Hamilton's regional art gallery. Reg was also closely involved in getting Swan Hill going, first with a small gallery on the riverboat *Gem* and then later with the Pioneer Settlement. Likewise Benalla: his friend Laurie Ledger, a Benalla agriculturalist and businessman, had been collecting Australian art for many years and didn't know what to do with it. Reg was horrified to see many of the valuable paintings hanging on the walls of Ledger's shearing shed. He suggested offering the lot to the Benalla City Council. Ledger made the offer, only to be rejected by the council on grounds of costs, of there being nowhere to house the collection and the old theme of 'what do we need art for?' Ledger was infuriated, but Reg talked him into paying a large sum to build a new gallery and convinced the Bolte government to provide matching funds. The council finally weighed in behind the project and Benalla got its fine regional gallery.

As the Melbourne Arts Centre building progressed, Reg insisted it have a lounge for country visitors and began to argue for regional performing theatres as well as art gallery funding. He played a key role, too, in the development of the Geelong Performing Arts Centre. He wrote to the premier, Rupert Hamer, in 1969, flagging a more coordinated approach to all the arts across Victoria, with the building of performing arts centres alongside art galleries in regional areas.

> Responsible people with a knowledge of art galleries overseas express the view that nowhere in the world is there in evidence a complex of galleries with the potential for servicing the complete area of a state than exists in the state of Victoria. I am of the opinion that a similar situation is possible of achievement in the field of the performing arts. It is fortunate that at this

time there has been formed in Victoria a branch
of the Arts Council of Australia, whose field of
activity lies almost entirely in provincial areas. It
is commendable that the State Government has
seen fit to recognise this practically by way of a
financial annual grant.

Reg was also key to Mildura's most famous
contribution to the arts in Australia—the Mildura
Sculpturescapes. Initiated by Ernst van Hattum, the first
director of the Mildura Arts Centre, in 1961, this event
grew to become the major sculpture event in Australia.
The experimental works caused controversy in the city as
many locals were baffled by what they were seeing. I can
remember my father coming home bemused, describing
one artist, 'sitting on a swing, naked, swinging from the
stage of the arts centre, pissing on the audience!'

The sculpturescapes were so confronting to some
Mildura citizens they determined they would do all
they could to undermine Reg, and ultimately he was
kicked off council at an election. He then began a new
project raising money to reconstruct the First Mildura
Homestead.

The original Mildura Homestead was occupied by
the Chaffey brothers above the red cliffs of the Murray
River when they began the irrigation settlement. Reg
chaired the Homestead Establishment Committee for 10
years. Although no longer a member of the council, he
knew where all the bodies were buried and he had many

allies from his time as mayor. When some councillors objected to any expenditure of ratepayer funds on the Homestead, Reg got work done unapproved by council. Workers came with council equipment and planted the rose garden at the Homestead and did other jobs unofficially. When council tried to stop work on the Homestead, Reg, as a rebel chairman, refused to call a meeting and work continued. He was a law unto himself and council could not stop him. He got funds through connections in Melbourne and in the end the building was completed and officially opened in 1984: it is now one of Mildura's tourist attractions. Reg would often say, 'Money is only a lubricant, that's all it is.' And that's the way he operated.

Running parallel with this activity in the arts, Reg had scientific interests. These involved his work for the Department of Post-War Reconstruction making the world's first wide-angle lenses for cameras used in Woomera rocket research, the basis of all inter-continental ballistic missiles and space rocketry since.

The impetus for this top-secret manufacturing derived from the British government's alarm at the V2 rocket attacks on London, and its realisation after atomic bombs fell on Hiroshima and Nagasaki that nuclear warheads could be attached to the new missiles. Winston Churchill had bombed the German rocket-manufacturing base at Peenemünde, dispersing the V2 enterprise, and at the end of the war there was a race by the US, Russia and Britain to capture the rocket scientists and obtain the new technology. Britain missed out, so decided to start its own work on missile development. In 1946 the Evatt Report recommended setting up the Salisbury Weapons' Research Establishment (WRE) and developing a vast rocket range at Woomera in South Australia. The climate of the Cold War and the Korean War of 1950 led Prime Minister Chifley to insist, despite British resistance, that Australia be part of British scientific rocket research and by 1951 Salisbury had started work on the pilotless Jindivik aeroplane. Rocket testing at Woomera was in full swing.

As one of Victoria's first qualified optometrists, and because of his connections with R.D. Elliott and his work with the Minor Industries War Agricultural Committee, Reg was asked by the Department of Post-War Reconstruction to tour optical factories in Britain and the US. He was at the time District Governor for Rotary International, covering the whole of Victoria, South Australia and Western Australia. On his return to Australia in 1949, Reg was contracted by the Department of Supply to make optical lenses for a range of military uses: telescopic and rifle sights, and then Askania theodolytes, which were used to track missiles fired from the Woomera Rocket Range. He recruited skilled lens grinder Stan Johnson from Melbourne, was supplied with equipment to use in a small Mildura workshop and set up Etherington Optical in a Nissan hut behind a

Chinese restaurant he owned in Langtree Avenue.

In 1954, an Australian named Frank Dixon at the WRE invented the world's first wide-angle lens, the 'fish-eye' lens. It was unique because it could take a 360-degree photo, thus enabling rockets to see over the horizon. As such it marked the beginning of the new age of inter-continental ballistic missiles, an age that led to the fear of nuclear attack and Reagan's Star Wars program, aimed at stopping any future attack from space on the United States. It was this wide-angle lens that made Etherington Optical a top-secret production facility. To make full use of the rocket range and this lens, scientists invented the new WRECISS and WRETAR cameras, one attached to the nose of a target Jindivik and the other to the missile being launched against it.

The wide-angle lenses were manufactured in Mildura along with prisms, optical blanks, rifle telescopic sights, submarine and tank periscope lenses, binocular and range-finder lenses. In 1954 Reg had applied to the minister, Black Jack McEwan, for a glass import licence and foresaw the potential for a world-class optical manufacturing industry for Australia. By 1959, Etherington Optical was in full production, but it was a frustrating experience. Bureaucratic bungles led to equipment delivery delays, supply of faulty glass slabs, inefficient grinding machines, incorrect specification for some lenses, and unnecessary rejection of 'faulty work'.

By 1958–59, Britain was secretly testing guided nuclear missiles. But because they were being left behind by Russia and the USA (with its sky-to-air 'Skybolt' missile) and because there was unease in Britain and NATO at the escalation of the arms race, Britain withdrew. This left Etherington Optical high and dry.

Never easily daunted, Reg wrote to the Department of Supply in 1961 arguing that this industry was a vital one for Australia. The bureaucratic and political establishment seemed unable to appreciate the future potential and lost the opportunity to keep Australia at the forefront of optical and missile research and manufacturing. Reg closed down his Mildura plant and Stan Johnson left for Salisbury.

Reg contained his significant disappointment and continued with all his other projects. There was an aura around him. He exuded confidence. I never saw him indecisive or intimidated. He was called upon for advice in many capacities, by all sorts of people, about how to get things done. At the age of 72, when JPs were normally expected to retire, a group of leading citizens of Mildura applied for his reinstatement to the Royal Victorian Association of Honorary Justices, describing him as an 'Indefatigable member of numerous organisations with a wonderful knowledge and history of the district and its people. One of the most respected members of the community still active and influential... Many people half his age would be happy to have his mental agility and understanding of issues.'

My father was a visionary whose acumen and strategy I learned to appreciate. While I had absorbed political skills just growing up in a household with him, I turned to him first when I was faced with difficult decisions and he usually gave me invaluable advice. He taught me to think big. If something was worth doing then you went for the full caboodle. He also taught me not to take myself too seriously. He used to say, 'Don't let your wishbone grow where your funny bone ought to be.'

I got involved in the politics of change through studying the media, developing the first courses on film in an Australian university and reforming and producing children's television. My father would say to me, to my great irritation, 'Be patient, Patricia.' It took me many years to understand the value of that advice. I did learn in time that conflict is part of growth, that, as Dad believed, a strong community grows out of agreed and shared values which do not emerge spontaneously. It is necessary to argue and negotiate, but in a civil manner. Reg believed that serving the wider public good was a necessary complement to a satisfying private life.

He always found time for the family. When his grandchildren came along he spent time with each one of them. Without exception they enjoyed his company. 'You can't buy them with a cheque book,' he would say. Reg would take them camping and fishing, where with unending patience he would bait their hooks and find a fish to attach to their line if they hadn't caught one themselves. He would take them in his jeep down to the paddock where he bred cattle, with his dog Bingo. They would stop at the corner store to buy a bottle of 'red' (soft drink) and a bag of lollies. Often he had no money on him so Eva would go and pay the bill later. He would work away, digging his irrigation channels, mending fences and checking out his cows while the kids amused themselves playing in the dirt.

> There was a bloke who had a farm near my property. He used to come and watch me work hard all day in the sun, just standing there looking at me. One day he said, 'That land is no good for anything. You're mad.' I said, 'Yes, I'm mad and that's why you ride a bike and I drive a Buick. Now you go to buggery.'

My daughters remember him laughing his head off when they invented new words to sing to the Sunday school hymn, 'Jesus Wants Me for a Sunbeam'. Once he killed a tiger snake and brought it home to Sarnia Avenue. My two daughters helped him to arrange it, lifelike, on the path outside the kitchen door. They then called me to come from inside. I rushed out and saw the snake and yelled at them to 'Stand back!' while they collapsed in laughter and I realised I'd been set up. He once said the hardest thing about bringing up a family is learning to keep your mouth shut. Sometimes he succeeded and sometimes not.

In his late eighties, when Reg had ceased to be active in community affairs—a loss he felt very keenly—his project became my mother Eva. She had lost her mobility, while his years of hobby farming had kept him physically fit. She had held the household together, enabling Reg to be out day and night on his committees, and he knew he could not have achieved all he had without her support. She also played an important role in the community. He owed her, and in their final years together she became his purpose for being and Eva rather enjoyed the attention. They operated as a team as they had always done; she could tell Reg where everything was and remind him what he was trying to do and he could physically accomplish all that needed to be done. He was well into his eighties before he stopped climbing on the house roof to keep up repairs.

But he was losing his memory and Eva was concerned about how they would manage. He tried to conceal the extent of his problems from his daughters and would become hostile when challenged about whether he and Eva should remain in their home or move to supported residential care. As in most things, in the end he was right to insist they remain at home. Eva said she wanted to move but would not stand up to him nor would she make any decision independently of him. He remained in charge and it was too late to change that. The doctor insisted they were managing. Reg remained extraordinarily strong-willed and lost none of his psychological strength, despite failing in other ways. The doctor brought in an assessment team to make changes to the physical environment so Eva could move about more easily; they had meals on wheels and a housekeeper to clean and wash the laundry and Reg took care of the organisation of food and the house.

In March 1998 my mother had a stroke and was critically ill. She died within two weeks at the age of 89. She had had remarkably good health throughout her life with only three stays in hospital—for the birth of her third child, to remove her appendix and for rehabilitation after a bladder infection. She owed the health system nothing. Each day Reg walked to and from the hospital to sit with her; he wouldn't call a taxi. He held himself together and took charge of the funeral arrangements. Eva was buried in a plot in the Mildura cemetery bought some years before: 'the best piece of land in the cemetery. I paid 30 quid for it, a lot of money for those days.'

With Eva gone Reg changed. He had no cause for hostility towards his daughters anymore and he became a gentle, courteous person who still insisted on living alone, taking care of himself in the house he moved into when he married. He liked to see his family but he was not interested in social visits and conversation from any other well-meaning people. When visitors came to his door he told them not to return. His friends were dead and he didn't want new ones. He had always been a self-contained person and he was content with the security and familiarity of his own environment. He was pragmatic about his situation at 93; his life had centred on civic duty and that stage was over. 'I get lonely. I'm not talking about depression, but psychologically. You sit there at two o'clock and think, will I have a sleep? I might or I mightn't. Then it's five o'clock and I think I may as well eat and then go to bed.'

I never heard Reg complain about his lot. I spoke to him regularly from Melbourne by phone but saw him only when I could visit Mildura or on his twice-yearly visits to Melbourne. During one visit to Mildura my sister and I decided we would take him on a trip to Broken Hill. Reg was happy in the car but once we arrived at our motel he did not know where he was, who we were or how he would get home. We toured the galleries and the city and when we returned him home and I was back in Melbourne I phoned Dad to ask how he enjoyed his trip. He replied that he had but, 'Who were those two women who took me there?'

Despite memory loss Reg resisted any attempt to move him into a facility where he would have had company. But circumstances got the better of him, and once in care it did not take long before his life ended; he died within a year, at the age of 95.

Reg was a vital, active, engaged and interesting man

all his life. Like others in this book he had energy to burn; he had the intellectual capacity to reinvent himself at different stages of life; he was driven by desire to build a community and he was courageous both mentally and physically. He accomplished more than most people and he enjoyed the effort. A challenge fired him up. The anthropologist Margaret Mead is widely attributed with saying: 'Never doubt that a small group of thoughtful, committed citizens can change the world. Indeed it is the only thing that ever has.' Reg Etherington was one of those people.

NOTES

CHAPTER 1

1. Simone de Beauvoir, *The Coming of Age*, W. W. Norton & Co., New York, 1970.
2. Pat Thane, ed., *The Long History of Old Age*, Thames & Hudson, London, 2005.
3. Donald Hall, 'Out the Window', *New Yorker*, 23 January 2012.
4. Clancy Yeates, 'Boomers Blowing Their Super to Pay Down Large Debts', *Age*, 3 October 2012.
5. Kate Legge, 'When Duty Calls', *Weekend Australian Magazine*, 2 June 2012.
6. Australian Bureau of Statistics, *Australian Social Trends*, 1996, cat. no. 6204.0.
7. In general, married men will live longer than single men but Aboriginal men and women will die 20 years earlier than other Australians. The gains in life expectancy are not distributed equitably. In New South Wales, for example, males born in the highest socio-economic status (SES) groups in 2007 are expected to live 4.3 years longer than those born in the lowest SES group, and an average of about 3.7 years longer than those born into the middle three SES groups. In females, the difference in life expectancy between the highest and lowest SES groups was 2.6 years in New South Wales in 2007. For the 12 years between 1995 and 2007, life expectancy increased for all SES groups for both males and females. The increase was greater for males than for females across SES groups. In absolute terms, the gap in life expectancy between the lowest and highest SES groups increased over this period. The difference in life

expectancy increased from 3.1 to 4.3 years for males, and from 1.6 to 2.6 years for females in New South Wales (www.healthstats.nsw.gov. au/Indicator/ses_lomidhilex).

In Britain, life expectancy rose over the last three decades for all social classes, but a persistent difference remained (in fact increased) between those on higher incomes and the disadvantaged. The highest life expectancy was for professional and managerial classes (80.4 years) and the lowest was for those in 'routine' and unskilled occupations (74.6 years). This can largely be put down to a difference in living conditions, housing, food and safety at work, the lower classes having always been in more hazardous occupations and more stressful, less healthy living conditions (www.statistics. gov.uk/hub/population/deaths/life-expe).

In the United States, there was a 19.6-year gap in life expectancy between the longest living group (Asian females, 84.9 years) and the shortest living (African-American males, 65.3 years). African-American males living in the poorest 20 per cent of California neighbourhoods had life expectancy comparable to that reported for males living in developing countries. Neighbourhood SES represents a readily available metric for ongoing surveillance of health disparities in the US. (fadelibrary.wordpress.com/2007/10/25/varia-tions-inli; www.ncbi.nlm.nih.gov/pmc/articles/PMC284987).

CHAPTER 2

1. Lin Hatfield Dodds, 'Aged Care Needs a Makeover', *Age*, 24 January 2011; Michael O'Neill, 'Innovative Ideas Are Required to Fund Aged Care', *Australian*, 24 January 2011; Adele Horin and Michelle Grattan, 'Aged Care Cost to Rise under Plan', *Age*, 9 August 2011.

2. Derek McMillan, 'Politics Not Policy, Is Dictating How Older Australians Live out Their Lives', *Age*, 27 December 2012.

3. Julia Medew, 'Centenarian with No Time to Get Old', *Age*, 20 August 2012.

4. John McCormack's interest in centenarians dates from 1995, and he published the first article on centenarians in Australia in the *Australasian Journal on Ageing* in 2000. He also maintains an informal list of the oldest people, including the oldest veteran, in Australia.

5. John McCormack, *The Longevity Revolution: The Emergence of Centenarians and Super-centenarians in Australia*, Bluechip Publishing, Sydney, 2012.

6. Heather Booth, 'The Changing Face of the Australian Population: growth in centenarians', *Medical Journal of Australia*, 2009 (3).

7. James Frost, 'Greying Is the Biggest Threat', *Australian*, 4 August 2012.

8. Michael Short, 'Go Forth and Multiply—and Regenerate', *Age*, 1 October 2012.

9. Dan Harrison, 'Cancer Programs Given a Boost', *Age*, 15 May 2013. In the May 2013 Budget the age range for breast cancer screening was expanded to include women aged 70–74.

10. Articles such as Ian Munro, Farah Farouque, 'Shades of Grey', *Age*, 13 June 2012; 'The Demographic Time Bomb', *Age*, 8 January 2011; 'The Longevity Risk', *Melbourne University Magazine*, June 2010, are indicative.

11. Gary Banks, Chairman of the Productivity Commission, Health Policy Oration, John Curtin School of Medical Research, ANU, Canberra, June 2008.

12. Daniel Klein, *Travels with Epicurus*, Text Publishing, Melbourne, 2012.

13. Sian Powell, 'When It's Time', *Weekend Australian Magazine*, 8 September 2012.

14. Kate Hagan, 'Cholesterol Drugs Also Good for Low Risk Patients', *Age*, 6 August 2012.

15. Stephen Duckett, *Australia's Bad Drug Deal: High Pharmaceutical Prices*, Grattan Institute Report, Melbourne, March 2013.

16. A study in 2008 by Deloitte Economics reported the net economic benefits from avoided adverse drug reactions and unnecessary pharmaceutical spending alone would be between $2.5 billion and $6.2 billion over five years once the science was fully implemented. The cash-strapped health system has the potential to save $12 billion over the next five years and improve dramatically the lives of many patients, yet doesn't do so. Neil Batt, 'A Scandal That Wastes Billions and Does Harm', *Age*, 10 February 2011.

17. Al Gore, *The Future: Six Drivers of Social Change*, Random House, New York, 2013.

18. Julia Medew, 'Push for tougher line on surgery', *Age*, 4 October 2012.

19. Michael D. Coory, 'A Study of Ageing and Health Care Costs in

Australia: A Case of Policy-based Evidence', *The Medical Journal of Australia*, 2004.

20. Norman Swan, Breakfast, Radio National, 15 April 2013.
21. Amy Corderoy, 'Statistics Reveal How Life Determines Death', *Age*, 29 December 2012.
22. Gretchen Reynolds, 'How to Jog Your Memory', *Age*, 22 April 2013.
23. Annie Rahilly, 'Ageing well', *Voice, The University of Melbourne, Age*, 8 April 2013.
24. Amy Corderoy, 'Dementia Centre to Change Treatment', *Age*, 9 April 2013.
25. Norman Swan, Breakfast, Radio National, 17 September 2012.
26. Bernard Keane, 'The Rise and Rise of Health Spending—But Don't Blame Old People', Grattan Institute Report, *The Conversation*, 24 April 2013.
27. Mischa Merz, 'Lazy, Unmotivated...and Sloppy', *Age*, 3 October 2012.
28. Peter Beattie, 'A Big Fat Problem That Is a Greater Killer Than Smoking', *Weekend Australian*, 4 August 2012.
29. Katherine Burton, 'US Young Warned: Beware the Seniors', *Age*, 4 March 2013.
30. Padma Iyer, 'Age-old Stereotype Must Go', *Weekend Australian*, 2 March 2013.
31. Ben Schneiders, 'Researcher Astounded by Award at Age 91', *Age*, 13 June 2011.
32. Annie Rahilly, 'Girl's own Adventure', *voice.unimelb.edu.au*.
33. 'Monetary Scholar of Great Influence', Obituary, *Age*, 5 September 2012.
34. 'Lauded US Author Expanded the Reach of History', Obituary, *Age*, 12 November 2012.
35. Julia Medew, 'Centenarian with No Time to Get Old', *Age*, 20 August 2012.
36. Kevin Cool, 'The Last of a Class', *Stanford*, January/February 2013.
37. *The Sun*, 'Sunbeams', Issue 431, November 2011.
38. Tim Colebatch, 'Secrets to Ageing Gainfully', *Age*, 8 January 2011.
39. C. Milward, *Understanding links between family experience, obligations and expectations in later life*, Working Paper 19, AIFS, Melbourne, 1998; C. Milward, *Family Relations and Intergenerational Exchange in Later Life*,

Working Paper 15, AIFS, Melbourne, 1998.

40. David de Vaus, Matthew Gray and David Stanton, *Measuring the Value of Unpaid Household Caring and Voluntary Work of Older Australians*, AIFS Research Report, No.34, Melbourne 2003.

41. Ross Gittins, 'Simple Fact is We Spend Insufficient Time with Family', *Age*, 13 March 2013.

42. Tim Colebatch, 'Working Late: Grey Force for New Age,' *Age*, 18 May 2013.

43. Tim Colebatch, 'Australia's Coming of Age', *Age*, 11 September 2012.

44. Tim Colebatch, 'Working Longer, Retiring Stronger', *Age*, 9 February 2012.

45. Bianca Hall, 'Dismantling Begins on Barriers for Older Workers', *Age*, 3 October 2012.

46. Peter Martin, 'Figures Add up for Mature-age Workers in Jobs', *Age*, 3 September 2012.

47. Mihaly Csikszentmihalyi, *Flow: The Psychology of Optimal Experience*, Harper Perennial, New York, 1991.

48. Anne-Maree Moodie, 'Hiring Older Is Wiser', *Age*, 8 September 2012.

CHAPTER 3

1. Bernard Salt, 'Aged and Aborigines Miss out on Internet in Wired Brown Land', *Australian*, 4 October 2012.

2. Ian Davis, 'A Toast to Life', *Sunday Age*, 9 September 2012.

3. John Banville, *Ancient Light*, Viking, London, 2012.

CHAPTER 4

1. Patricia Edgar and Hilary McPhee, *Media She*, William Heineman, Melbourne, 1974.

2. Gough Whitlam, *Age*, 25 August 1973.

3. ABC, 'Ageing Well', Encounter, Radio National.

4. 'Joining the World's Age-Friendly Communities', *Fifty Plus, News*, April 2013.

5. Suzanne Carbone, 'A Very Good Read', *Age*, 7 May 2013.

6. Kate Legge, 'Parsley, Age, Miriam and Time', *Weekend Australian Magazine*, 1 May 2010.

7. *Health and Science News*, The week, 14 May 2010.

8. Jane Richards, 'Life at 100. It Only Gets Better', *Age*, 4 March 2013.
9. George E. Vaillant, *Ageing Well: Surprising Guideposts to a Happier Life from the Landmark Harvard Study of Adult Development*, Little Brown, 2003.
10. Christopher Croke, 'Proof Positive That Things Can Get Better', *Weekend Australian*, 9 February 2013.
11. Dan Buettner, 'Blue Zones', *Weekend Australian Magazine*, 2 February 2013.
12. Simone de Beauvoir, op. cit.
13. Anthony Burgess, 'The Clockwork Condition', *New Yorker*, 4 and 11 June 2012.
14. Weekender, *Age*, 19 February 2001.
15. Paul Auster, *Winter Journal*, Faber and Faber, London, 2012.
16. William Ian Miller, *Losing It*, Yale University Press, 2011.
17. Michael Leunig, 'The Warm Heart in Winter', *Age*, 29 May 2010.
18. Kate Legge, op. cit., 1 May 2010.

ADDITIONAL REFERENCES:

Mary Catherine Bateson, *Composing a Further Life: The Age of Active Wisdom*, Knopf, 2010.

Don Edgar, 'Star Wars and Australia's Secret Past', 2003, www.patricia-edgaranddonedgar.com.

Erik H. Erikson and Joan Erikson, *The Life Cycle Completed*, W.W. Norton & Co., New York, 1997.

ACKNOWLEDGEMENTS

I WANT TO OFFER my sincere gratitude to those who shared their stories, inspiring me to write about ageing. This book is dedicated to my parents, Reg and Eva Etherington, who I thought would go on forever. They first demonstrated to me that life was to be lived until the end with enthusiasm and optimism. Lesley Falloon was my poster-girl who led me to write her story and seek others like her. Flora Noyce, Mary Owen, Jim Brierley, John Tucker, John Lovell and Muriel Crabtree have all been great company through this process and admirable advocates for a long life well lived. I thank you all for your involvement and support.

I am most fortunate to be working with Text Publishing. The wise Michael Heyward leads an exemplary team. From the very first meeting, when I learnt all involved at Text had already read my manuscript and were enthusiastic and committed, this has been a professional and most enjoyable process, and I thank all I have worked with in the Text team. I was fortunate to have Michael as my editor. His clear vision for the book, along with his encouragement, has led to a happy and productive collaboration. Rachel Shepheard and Michelle Calligaro in publicity and promotions have also been a delight to work with. I thank W.H. Chong for his elegant design and Rebecca Starford for her meticulous overseeing of the manuscript.

I particularly want to acknowledge Don Edgar, my husband and partner in all things I do, for his incisive critical comments, involvement and support from concept to completion. I also thank my daughters Sue Amoddio and Lesley Edgar, as well as Adrian Mills for their comments on the manuscript. I am grateful to Dr Geoff McColl who assisted my understanding of the drug approval process in Australia.

I must also thank my readers who I trust will help change perceptions and understanding of ageing.